BEYOND RELIGION

Beyond Religion

The Truth and Error in
'Religionless Christianity'

Thomas

DANIEL JENKINS

The Westminster Press

PHILADELPHIA

Library of Congress Catalog Card No.: 64-13758

CONTENTS

PREFACE

THIS book is a considerably revised version of the Laidlaw lectures delivered at Knox College in the University of Toronto in 1957. It was a very great privilege to be present at this historic college during its centenary celebration, to receive one of its honorary degrees and to enjoy its generous hospitality.

I am grateful to the Reverend David Edwards for many editorial suggestions, and to Simon Jenkins for preparing the index.

February 1962   D. J.

PUBLISHER'S NOTE

DR JENKINS contributes his reactions to the Bishop of Woolwich's book *Honest to God* in *The Honest to God Debate* (October 1963).

I

The Present Interest in 'Religionless Christianity'

'R ELIGIONLESS Christianity' is in danger of becoming a catch-phrase, at least in those small but influential circles where new ideas are given their first airings. Like most catch-phrases, it is used more to indicate an awareness that an interesting set of notions exists which might bear further examination than to define something which is clearly formulated and easily recognizable. These notions express the belief that mature Christian faith can exist independently of the religious activities with which it has always been closely associated and that, although this is more debatable, this is the only form in which it can exist for many people today. Discussion of them started as a result of some brief observations made along these lines by Dietrich Bonhoeffer, in letters written from prison before his martyrdom at the hands of the Nazis.[1] As yet, they have been no more than the subject of essays and articles and informal conversation, and no one can point to a school of thought or a movement which uses 'religionless Christianity' as its watchword. The character of the conversation is such, however, as to suggest that a school of thought or movement of this kind might easily emerge.

[1] *Letters and Papers from Prison*, 1953 (SCM Press; rev. ed. 1956; also in Fontana paperbacks, Collins; American ed. *Prisoner for God*, Macmillan). See esp. pp. 122-7, 145-9, 162-4, 168-9. Some passages are given in an Appendix to this book, by permission of the holders of the copyright.

This makes it opportune that some modest effort should be made to promote the more sustained discussion of the circle of ideas related to 'religionless Christianity'. I believe that these ideas are of great practical importance. It is very doubtful, however, whether they are accurately described by such terms as 'religionless Christianity', and most of the people who are convinced of their importance would probably prefer to use different terms in speaking of them. They also have connections, which it should be useful to make clear, with other important ideas with which they are not readily associated. And the interest which they arouse comes from widely differing quarters and is produced by widely differing causes. These need to be carefully distinguished from one another if confusion is to be avoided.

1. *Why are People Interested?*

This last point may be the simplest with which to begin. 'Religionless Christianity' and the idea which we shall see to be very closely linked with it, that of 'God above God', has aroused some interest among those people, of whom there are very many in the academic world, who confess to a measure of attachment to the Christian faith but who have no overt commitment to it and who are deeply distrustful of the organized churches. This is partly, no doubt, because they may think of it as a new form of an interpretation of Christianity to which people of self-consciously liberal outlook have always felt themselves attracted—an interpretation which is theologically and ethically generalized, and which sees little need for the Church as a clearly defined community. But this interest may also be due to an eagerness to give attention to a fresh interpretation of the Christian faith which is not open to the objections which these people feel compelled to make to most of the interpretations with which they are familiar. Professor Perry Miller has spoken[1] of 'the intense delight with which students come to the end of Paul Tillich's *The Courage To Be* when they read his declaration that we must seek the God beyond the God', and how he sees that act of seeking as the achievement of true freedom. Too much must not be made of this since it was only a brief observation, although expressed in a form which suggested that it was not lightly made, but it certainly underlines the importance of knowing what we are talking about when we move into this circle of ideas. The borderline between the genuinely self-critical attitude which is able to break through into true faith and the merely self-centred attitude which is more concerned with its own good opinion of itself than with the truth is always narrow, as we all know from our experience of ourselves, and it is at its narrowest over this part of the theological field.

On the other hand, the circles in which 'religionless Christianity' and its related ideas have aroused the greatest and the most animated interest are very different from these. They are those of people who would be considered by ordinary standards to be notably 'religious' Christians, professional theologians and exceptionally well informed lay leaders of the churches. What is more, among these they have often been those who have been most vocal in asserting the uniqueness and distinctiveness of the revelation of God in Christ, as recorded in Scripture and as proclaimed by the Church. It is true that most of them would probably want to say that they thought 'religionless Christianity' was a misleading expression and that they would prefer another. They would agree that Christian faith without its accompanying religion is an impossibility in terms of life upon this earth. But they would also want to assert that religion,

---

[1] In *Religion and Freedom of Thought*, 1954 (SCM Press and Doubleday), p. 21.

even when it bears a Christian name, is a highly ambiguous
activity and can quickly become faith's greatest enemy. This
is particularly true when it is a noble religion which bears
many marks of being the good fruit of past faith. True faith,
they would say, always needs to go beyond religion if it is
to justify men in God's sight.

This critique of religion from the side of faith has developed in two directions. The first has been through the
critical theological examination of religion itself in the light
of Christian revelation. Here the outstanding name is that of
Karl Barth. As long ago as the second half of the first
volume of his *Church Dogmatics*, Barth headed a chapter
with the words 'The Revelation of God as the Abolition of
Religion', and he frequently pointed out the dangers of
religion in his commentary on the Epistle to the Romans.
Barth's influence upon Bonhoeffer was very great and frequently acknowledged, and the train of thought which led
Bonhoeffer to develop his ideas about 'religionless Christianity' can be easily followed. Hendrik Kraemer also related some of Barth's insights about religion to the discussion of the place of Christian faith among the religions of
the world, including the 'Christian religion', in his influential book, *The Christian Message in a non-Christian World*
(1938). He restated his position in a manner somewhat more
critical of Barth in his later book, *Religion and Christian
Faith* (1956).[1]

The other direction in which this critique has moved has
been the result of a difference of interest rather than of attitude, for it has been substantially the same theological position which has been involved in both. Those making it have
emphasized that faith does not mean primarily the cultiva-

---

[1] See also a highly generalized treatment of a related theme,
Radical Monotheism and Western Culture, by H. R. Niebuhr, 1960
(Faber and Harper).

tion of the religious affections, no matter how refined or elaborate or edifying the manner in which this may be done, but that it does mean obedience to God in action in the world in which all men find themselves, the so-called 'secular' world. Here the most influential spokesman has been Dietrich Bonhoeffer, although his early death at the hands of the Nazis in 1945 prevented him from adequately working out his ideas. All, in fact, that he has left with us which deals directly with the subject are the few pages of his letters from prison which were mentioned at the outset. Some of the implications of his ideas can, however, be traced in his unfinished book on *Ethics* (Eng. trans. 1955).[1] These ideas are being followed up most vigorously by those connected with the World Council of Churches who are trying to work out a fresh approach to the task of the laity in the Church, notably by H. H. Walz and Hans-Ruedi Weber. Hendrik Kraemer has also shown an active concern for these matters, both as first director of the Ecumenical Institute at Bossey and in his recent book on *The Theology of the Laity* (1958). A short book by Ronald Gregor Smith, *The New Man* (1956), was directly inspired by Bonhoeffer and it has also underlined the affinity of these ideas with those of the men of the Reformation.

The catch-phrase most readily associated with this side of the critique has been 'holy worldliness', which was given currency in an article with that title by Alec Vidler.[2] This phrase is as inviting as 'religionless Christianity' but, if anything, even more misleading. Indeed, to anyone with less than a German delight in paradox it is an extremely bewildering expression. Holiness in the Bible is a quality

[1] See John D. Godsey, *The Theology of Dietrich Bonhoeffer*, 1960 (SCM Press and Westminster Press, Philadelphia).
[2] Reprinted in his *Essays in Liberality*, 1957 (SCM Press).

which derives only from God, and in relation to men and to natural objects it is bound up with the idea of separation. It is true that 'the world' is used in several senses in the New Testament, but it is perhaps most characteristically thought of as existence apart from God, lying in the hands of the evil one, passing away to nothingness and needing to be overcome by the victory of faith. It is the mark of believers that they live in the world as those who are not of it. Yet although 'holy worldliness' is a phrase which must seem confusing rather than illuminating to anyone concerned to maintain the integrity of the language of the New Testament, the idea which it is trying to express is of the greatest importance. The main thesis of this book will be that these two closely related ideas of the need for an internal critique of religion from the point of view of faith, and of the need to move beyond religion into faithful action in the midst of this present world, are of the greatest importance in helping the Christian community in the Western world to recognize and define the most urgent tasks which confront it.

This is a large claim, and its justification will not become apparent unless, as does not always happen, these two ideas are held closely together and interpreted in a positive and constructive fashion. One of the difficulties which stand in the way of our doing this is created by the temperament and method of working of the man who has been most responsible for the re-introduction of these ideas into theology, Karl Barth. Despite the enormous bulk of his writing—perhaps itself a hindrance rather than an aid to understanding in the English-speaking world—few theologians lend themselves to misinterpretation more readily than he. This is partly because the immense power of his theological genius is concentrated all the time on one theme, and that a theme of the utmost importance, the maintenance of the initiative of God the sovereign Lord in the revelation of himself as against all the efforts of men to wrest that initiative from him. This always makes Barth far more concerned to detect and to repel every possible threat to the sovereignty of God in his revelation than to try to define carefully the relation between that revelation and the other parts of human experience and knowledge. Misunderstanding also arises partly, perhaps, because of Barth's genially polemical method of writing, which makes him take for granted elements of truth in the positions of those with whom he disagrees and fasten on the points of disagreement. These serve to conceal the extent to which the motive lying behind Barth's approach is a liberating and constructive one, which may indeed turn out to have more points of affinity with the more sincere forms of so-called non-religious interest in 'religionless Christianity' which were mentioned earlier than superficial observation might suggest. That this may well prove to be the case is indicated not only by Barth's sympathy with radical ecclesiastical and political views but also by the notorious 'liberalism' of his doctrine of man, especially as exemplified in the third volume of his *Church Dogmatics*.[1] Some of his bewildered critics have alleged that this is inconsistent with what has gone before. It is not inconsistent, however, with his professed intention, although it has to be acknowledged that when he sallies forth after someone who appears to threaten his cherished central position all tends to be forgotten in the excitement of the chase.

For what Barth does by his constant emphasis upon the facts that faith must never be regarded as a work, and that religion (as man's effort to reach God or to respond to God) is not what saves him, is to provide room for genuine pro-

[1] See also his lecture on 'The Humanity of God'. Eng. trans. in the 1961 book of that title (Collins and John Knox Press).

phetic criticism of the Church from within and to release
men for self-forgetful service of God's will in the real world.
This is made increasingly clear in the fourth volume of his
Dogmatics. He underlines the truth that the Church's dead-
liest foes are those of her own household, and that the
condition of her faithful obedience to God is that she
should achieve genuine self-transcendence. He makes clear
what men find it peculiarly hard to accept, that the ambiguity of religion stands most startlingly revealed when it
is closest to the act of faith, because it is at that point that
our self-centred attitude is most radically threatened and, in
desperation, masquerades as true service of God in order
to save itself.

It is one of the purposes of this study to show how this
attempt to cut religion down to size at the very place where
it becomes most sure of itself provides the only reliable
basis for the criticism of the self-righteousness, with its
allied conservatism, displayed by institutions bearing a
Christian label, which is one of the chief hindrances to the
free movement of the Spirit in our own time. Judgment
begins at the house of God, and the corollary of that fact
is that the most searching and comprehensive criticism of
any church which understands the teaching of its Lord must
always come from within. It is only when the Church recognizes that faith lies beyond religion, as a gift from the Godward side to man, which judges the religion of the Church
as well as that of other communities and which can find
expression only in self-forgetting love, that it is in a position to use the only resources provided for it by its Lord to
prevent it from becoming conformed like any other institution to this world which passes away. Where this recognition is not made, the Church may rapidly become an impressive institution—indeed it may find it all the easier to
do so—but it will no longer be the servant of the divine

purpose. Its very religiousness will do no more than confirm and celebrate its secularization.

This insight exposes the superficiality of many of the
criticisms of Christian religious institutions made from the
outside by liberally-minded persons. These, of course, are
not necessarily the same as theological liberals. Theological
liberalism is now a very general term, which covers several
widely different points of view, and in speaking of liberals
here we are thinking chiefly of those numerous people in
Western society who are interested in, and not unsympa-
thetic towards, Christianity, but who are not associated with
the churches, and are often highly critical of them. Their
weakness, more in this realm than in any other, is their characteristic one of refusing to face the implications of engagement. The difficulties and hazards of the religious enterprise are at once more formidable and more inescapable
than they are prepared to envisage. They are the eager spec-
tators of the efforts of others to embark upon the stormy
seas of religious endeavour but regard themselves as free to
continue as men of independent judgment. They imagine
that they are entitled to approve or disapprove of the performance of the professedly religious man, for all the world
as though they were free from the necessities which con-
strain him. They are like the *phronimoi* described by Paul
in I Cor. 4.9, self-satisfied wiseacres who know all the
answers before they have begun honestly to face the questions, and who suppose that they do not have to undergo
the humiliation of making a spectacle of themselves, becoming a *theatron*, like the apostle. But they are deceived.
The only way in which religion can be effectively criticized
is from within. The reason for this is that the only criterion
for the criticism is that provided by God himself in faith.
This may seem unconvincing to the man who maintains
that he stands outside the situation in which he is addressed

by God but it has yet to be proved that any other criterion
for criticism can become effective. The uncommitted liberal
with his 'religionless' interest in Christianity has no means
for resolving the immense dilemmas created for the human
spirit by religion itself. The virtue of the religious criticism
of religion is that it has. It acknowledges the fact that, in
the strict sense, a 'religionless Christianity' is impossible
and that to be justified in God's sight a man has to come
to terms with his religion, has to commit himself un-
reservedly to the religious undertaking, and yet, realizing
fully the ambiguity of this enterprise, strive to transcend
himself in the act of faith working through love. More than
that, he has to accept the fact that faith, once he has found
it and given it expression in love, will nourish fresh religion
within him. This, in its turn, exposes him anew to the
danger of resting content with this situation, instead of continuing to struggle to the place where the venture of faith
has to be made in a new setting. To recognize that the fruit
of faith itself, in religion and in the works of love, stands in
need of constant reformation is the condition of his being
able genuinely to live the Christian life.

It is only in this context that the notion lying behind 'holy
worldliness' can be properly understood. Faith is a reality
beyond religion and there is a sense in which it is true that
it is only when a man has found release from the burden
of religion that he can find his true fulfilment and maturity
in self-forgetting service of God in the round of daily life.
In faith, he possesses not merely inward peace and reassur-
ance but the ability to express Christ's reconciling grace in
human relationships of every kind and also in his relation
to the natural world about him. He becomes one who
'realizes the universal human', in Kierkegaard's phrase, and
it is Kierkegaard who has given us the classic picture of
'holy worldliness' in the wonderful description of the

'knight of faith' in *Fear and Trembling*, who constantly makes the movements of infinity but 'does this with such correctness and assurance that he constantly gets the finite out of it'.[1] It is the same Kierkegaard who also produced the most savage and sustained denunciation of religion as the enemy of faith in his *Attack upon Christendom*.[2]

2. *The Importance of the Discussion*

In one sense, of course, all this is no more than the expression of a very familiar truth of the Christian faith, and those who recognize this may well wonder where its originality lies. That Christians should live in the midst of the world as those who are not of it, and that the Christian man is the truly integrated and mature human being, who finds freedom in the bond-service of Christ through overcoming the destructive power of the world—what could be more familiar than that? But the originality of this idea of 'holy worldliness' lies in its recognition of how subtle and many-sided are the efforts of religion to create barriers between faith and its realization. The originality lies also in the understanding of how complete an identification with the world in its need, and how great a power to overcome the world at its strongest, is possible for the man of faith.

Christian history is full of examples of the way in which this truth, clear and fundamental as it is, needs constantly to come with the freshness of new discovery to a Christian

---

[1] The whole passage in *Fear and Trembling*, quoted in an Appendix to this book, is well worthy of study from this point of view. The one thing which is significantly lacking is a picture of the knight in the relationship of love with his neighbour, which points to Kierkegaard's own failure to 'realize the universal human'.

[2] Eng. trans. 1944, from the Danish of 1854-5 (OUP and Princeton).

community which has forgotten or trivialized it. It is also full of examples of how quickly this truth can be forgotten or trivialized. Ronald Gregor Smith has reminded us that Luther gave classic expression to the truth which 'holy worldliness' is trying to convey in his *Address to the Nobility of the German Nation,* written in the first flush of the Reformation, when he said, 'The sphere of faith's works is worldly society and its order'.[1] This was solidly of a piece with his teaching about justification by faith, with his protest against the 'work-righteousness' of his time, and with his emphasis on the freedom of the Christian man. Luther's *Primary Works* are among the charter-documents of 'holy worldliness', and their liberating effect on Christian men in the modern world has been of enormous importance. This did not prevent Lutheranism from making false distinctions between the Church and the world, which have weakened its influence to this day. In this, it has been far from unique among churches. The record of the Reformed churches may be a little better in this particular respect but the difference is no more than one of slight degree. Various efforts have been made to re-capture and re-apply the insights of 'holy worldliness', especially since the second half of the nineteenth century, when men became increasingly aware of the extent to which an industrialized society appeared to be developing according to a law of its own without reference to any Christian criteria. One of the most determined of these was the Social Gospel movement in Protestantism of the early part of the twentieth century. The concern of this movement was admirable, and its achievements were not inconsiderable. But its weakness lay in its inadequate ideas both of the Kingdom of God and of human sinfulness, which prevented most of its exponents from dealing effectively either with the ambiguity of re-

[1] *The New Man,* p. 41.

ligion or with the problem of power in society. Today, largely under the influence of Reinhold Niebuhr, the problems of power in society are being more realistically faced, but Christians cannot expect to offer any distinctive insights for the solution of these problems unless they also recognize the need for the radical prophetic criticism of religious activities and institutions from within.[1]

Spokesmen for religious institutions are familiar enough with the dangers into which people run when they do not take their specifically religious activities seriously enough. Much of the energy of these spokesmen is directed towards keeping their fellows up to the mark in this respect. They have yet to see that the dangers of being led into a false other-worldliness by religion are no less great. This is not done, of course, simply by minimizing the importance of religious activity. It is essential that God's children should find time for withdrawal from secular occasions to concentrate more closely upon life's fulfilment in communion with God—particularly in an age so occupied with the surface of life as ours. But this withdrawal will be false unless it is clearly seen from the outset that its fruit is a greater identification in love with their neighbours in this present world. Experience shows that people find that it is good for them to be in the places to which they have temporarily withdrawn, and to occupy themselves with building tabernacles, with the result that they are unable to move forward in obedience to the will of God in the real world. When they do this, they find that they have not kept pace with their Lord, with the result that the place in which they find themselves is never truly the 'other world' in which he dwells. It is only one particular part of that world which lies under

---

[1] Reinhold Niebuhr's book *Pious and Secular in America*, 1957 (Scribner), underlines the truth of this. (British title: *Essays Godly and Ungodly*, Faber.)

the dominion of evil powers, a world of self-conscious religiousness and of institutions which bear pious labels. Their holy otherworldliness is, in fact, no more than one form of unholy worldliness.

It is important to recognize also that religious men are exposed to this temptation on profound as well as upon superficial levels of experience. The rounds of minor social activities which absorb so much of the time and activity of many ordinary churches are obviously ways of insulating them against their real duty in the real world. But the doctrinal rigidity of some forms of Protestantism, and the disproportionate sacramental preoccupation of many forms of Catholicism, can have the same effect. It is true that these more serious and disciplined religious attitudes do create more bracing surroundings for the encouragement of the venture of faith—but they can also more easily persuade people that the pursuit of their characteristic activities is identical with the venture of faith.

The protest on behalf of a right relationship to this present world on the part of the true servant of God is as necessary and as salutary today as it was in the time of Amos. God must be obeyed not merely in what men call the Church but also in what they call the world—in men's politics, business, industry and all the other spheres of human activity and association in which their lives are lived. And he must be obeyed not by considering how life in these spheres must be related to life in the institutions of the Church, nor by turning the questions which confront men in their living experience into 'religious' questions, nor even by raising the 'Christian' issue in relation to them in a self-conscious way. God must be obeyed by seeing his will in terms of the situations in which men find themselves. Any action taken by men of faith must certainly be action taken in the light of the fact that the God who raised Jesus

Christ from the dead is King over all life. This does not mean, however, that God lives only within that sphere designated by men as the religious, or that those who might reasonably claim to be experts in religion have the right because of this to speak authoritatively concerning the will of God for all the rest of life. The various spheres of human life have their own integrity, and the man with the religious vocation—the man whose eyes have been opened by faith to the ambiguity of the situation in which his vocation has placed him—will realize how careful he must be to respect that integrity. Secular institutions are dependent on God— in Paul Tillich's phrase 'heteronomous'—but they are meant to be independent, 'autonomous', in relation to ecclesiastical institutions in society, particularly when ecclesiastical institutions are represented by clergy and theologians. It need hardly be said that this does not mean that churches, clergy and theologians should have no relation to non-religious institutions. But it does mean that they should see very clearly that their function in relation to the 'secular' is one of ministry, not of secret lordship.

Once again, we are in danger of being misled by the method of the very man who can help us most, Karl Barth. Theology, to use another of Tillich's favourite phrases, deals primarily with matters related to man's 'ultimate concern'. It is the supreme merit of Barth as a theologian that, with unerring instinct, in any theological discussion, he fastens on the ultimate issue in relation to God as he has revealed himself in Christ. This attitude is of the greatest possible value in dealing with the central issues of theology, but it needs to be seen very carefully in relation to the rest of experience when matters of conduct in the world are being dealt with. Barth, as we have seen, is not always very interested in this relationship. Bonhoeffer, who in his general theological position is very close to Barth, is of greater help in this respect. He draws a distinction between 'the Last Things and the Things before the Last', and emphasizes the importance of the penultimate.[1] It is a deep insight of faith that before God all men are ultimately in the wrong, except in so far as they are covered with the righteousness of Christ. But that does not mean that, for immediate practical purposes, it is not important to recognize that certain actions are better, and worse, than others from our human point of view. On the contrary, our insight into the ultimate truth concerning man's moral state before God makes us more, and not less, sensitive to moral distinctions in the shifting circumstances of human life— since we see that some actions prepare the way for God's justification of the sinner, while others place obstacles before it. This is why, as Bonhoeffer says, we need to 'fortify the penultimate with a more emphatic proclamation of the ultimate, and also to protect the ultimate by taking due care for the penultimate'.

If the criticism of religion from the point of view of faith which Karl Barth, in particular, is helping the Church to make is to do the liberating work which it can do in our own time, it is essential that it be held in the closest connection with the set of ideas which are expressed in the term 'holy worldliness'. Eph. 4.11-17 makes it abundantly clear that the gifts of the Spirit are given to God's people not in order to shut them up in an enclosed world of their own, nor in order to produce a dictatorship of theologians over their brethren, but to enable all members of Christ to grow together into full maturity, into that 'proper man' who is able to deal truly in love in the midst of all the deceitfulness and confusion created by the powers of this present age. Unless it is clearly grasped from the outset that so-

[1] *Ethics*, pp. 79-100.

called 'religionless Christianity' is doing no more, and no less, than striving after a more adequate expression of faith working through love in maturity and freedom, it will remain on the level of an 'interesting' new idea which will become either frivolous or dangerously misleading.

II

Faith and Religion

WE have mentioned briefly the complicated nature of the relationship between true faith in God, as the New Testament understands it, and 'religion'. This relationship must now be looked at in more detail, since it is clearly of central importance for an enquiry into the truth and error of the ideas which are expressed in the phrase 'religionless Christianity'.

1. *Barth's Attack on Religion*

The theologian who has given most attention to this relationship is, as we have seen, Karl Barth, and he has done this most thoroughly in his extended discussion of 'The Revelation of God as the Abolition of Religion'.[1] Barth starts from the positive conviction, the implications of which few modern theologians have faced with such courage and honesty, that faith is the response to God's revelation of himself as Lord in Jesus Christ, a revelation in which the initiative rests firmly with God. Defining religion at this stage as man's quest for God, he says that if through religion man had been able to find God, this revelation would not have been necessary. That revelation has taken place proves religion's inadequacy, and now the whole field of religion must be looked at in the light of this fact. It is for this reason that the theologian does not start from the empirical study of 'religion'. Nor does he try, after the manner of neo-Protestantism (by which Barth means what is more commonly called Liberal Protestantism) to see how human re-

[1] *Church Dogmatics*, vol. i. 2, pp. 280-361 (T. and T. Clark, Edinburgh).

ligion and Christian faith can be co-ordinated. The theologian's task is to try to discover what the status of religion is from the point of view of faith.

Having made this characteristically definite and challenging statement at the outset of his discussion, Barth proceeds to qualify it and to safeguard it from misunderstanding. He does not, of course, deny the manifest universality of religion nor does he deny that faith arises out of the soil of human religion and is to be thought of as, in one sense, a religious act. He also emphasizes the need for charity and caution in the evaluation of religion. God does not speak to men through the Christian faith simply because in this faith Christians have somehow managed to create a better religion than anyone else. He speaks only because of his grace. The Christian man will see himself as a religious person like anyone else, who has yet been addressed by God and has had his religion overcome by God. To call religion 'unbelief' is not to show indifference to human greatness but it is, all the same, to see religion as the expression of the effort of godless man to make up for the lack of God on his own terms. In contrast to revelation, which is God's self-offering and self-manifestation, religion is 'a grasping which is not true reception'. 'If man believed, he would listen, but in religion he talks. If he believed, he would accept a gift; but in religion he takes something for himself. If he believed, he would let God himself intercede for God; but in religion he ventures to grasp at God' (p. 302). Barth does not specifically mention Phil. 2.6—where it is described as a peculiar mark of Christ's divine grace that, being in the form of God, he did not count it a thing to be greedily snatched at to be on an equality with God—but he would probably maintain that it bore out his contention.[1] This greedy snatching is a

[1] He does quote this passage in a not dissimilar context: *Church Dogmatics*, vol. ii. 2, p. 490.

mark of human religion and is an indication that the religious man does not, of himself, have within him 'that mind
which was in Christ Jesus'. The truth is that, apart from
faith, religion becomes idolatry, and Barth goes on to de-
scribe with great insight the way in which religion is thought
of as idolatry in the Bible (pp. 303-7).

Religion is unbelief also because it is man's attempt to
find justification and sanctification for himself on his own
terms. This is not the real way to God, but a self-centred
way of erecting barriers against him. Our characteristically
pious efforts to reconcile God to ourselves must indeed be
an abomination in his sight. 'Sin,' Barth says in a passage
which expresses the essence of his position on this matter
very clearly, 'is always unbelief. And unbelief is always
man's faith in himself. And this faith invariably consists in
the fact that man makes the mystery of his responsibility his
own mystery, instead of accepting it as the mystery of God.
It is this faith which is religion. It is contradicted by the
revelation attested in the New Testament, which is identical
with Jesus Christ as the one who acts for us and on us. This
stamps religion as unbelief' (p. 314).

Religion frequently recognizes its own imperfections and
tries to produce reactions against itself, which are protests
on behalf of a purer form of religion. One of these, according to Barth, is mysticism, and another, rather surprisingly,
is atheism, which, when it is serious, he sees as a basically
religious revolt against false religions. Yet these protests remain no more than special aspects of the self-confidence
which prompts men to embark upon their religious quest.
However hard they try, they cannot kill religion in its characteristic forms. The real crisis of religion only arises when
a quite new factor enters the situation, the divine action in
revelation.

Yet in all this violently negative thinking upon the subject of religion, Barth does not wish to suggest that no such thing as 'true religion' can exist. Revelation does not merely indict religion as unbelief; it also vindicates one kind of religion as pleasing in God's sight, that Christian religion which knows that it is possible to speak of 'true religion' only in the same way as it is possible to speak of a 'justified sinner'. The Christian religion becomes 'true' only as it is formed and sustained by divine revelation. The Bible must be read as an account for the struggle of revelation against the religion of revelation, a struggle in which the prophets do not spare prophecy itself. Here Barth's own prophetic illumination shines most brightly, in an eloquent passage in which he shows both how the history of Christianity can be thought of as the history of the disasters which Christianity creates for itself and how the strength of the believer is a 'strength made perfect in weakness' (pp. 331-3).

The truth of the Christian religion, Barth insists once more, is not to be found in any human characteristic it possesses as a historical movement; it is to be found only in the divine grace, focalized in the name of Jesus Christ. To bring out the full force of this claim, he contrasts the Christian religion with that of the Yodoist sect of Japanese Buddhism, which bears an astonishing resemblance to the religion of the Protestant Reformation, with the decisive qualification that it lacks Jesus Christ. Divine grace vindicates the Christian religion as true in so far as this religion is no more than the response in knowledge and worship to God's revelation in Christ poured out in the Spirit. In the same way, the Church exists as the Church not in so far as it possesses some inalienable human form but only as it lives by divine grace. Where it tries to create an animating principle of its own (p. 348), the Church ceases to be the Church of Jesus Christ and becomes an organ of that religion which is the enemy of faith.

Karl Barth is the most powerful of theologians, and the reader who has followed him all the way through is left stunned and breathless by the impact of his attack upon religion. But as soon as full awareness returns, we are left wondering whether the relation between religion and faith can be adequately dealt with only in these terms. Barth is undoubtedly calling attention to something of fundamental importance. What he says provides the basis for that internal criticism of the Christian religion which, as we shall see, is essential if it is to fulfil and not to resist the divine purpose. Yet it is regrettable that, in his avowedly systematic treatment of the matter, Barth should have allowed his polemical interest to over-ride every other consideration and to lead him to treat human religion in a one-sided and oversimple manner.

In doing this, Barth has inevitably proved himself unfaithful to his own best insights. The great strength of his position lies in his acceptance of the fact that, apart from the divine grace, the Christian religion becomes no more than one among the religions of the world. Religious activity under a Christian name provides no automatic assurance that it will be well-pleasing in God's sight. He does not make sufficiently clear, however, that the theologian himself can know no exemption from being confronted with this dilemma which all Christians have to deal with. It is surreptitiously taken for granted that when the Christocentric theologian speaks, his voice will carry the notes of authentic faith. That this is so is certainly far from Barth's frequently professed intention, from the commentary on the Epistle to the Romans onward. But that there is justice in this criticism is proved by the fact that he allows no real place for a dialogue between the representative of the Christian religion and those who think of religion in other terms. It is true that, as we have seen, he speaks of the need to show charity and caution in the evaluation of human religion and he makes the very important point that it is unreal to speak, as men have done, about human religion according to an abstract notion of 'the nature of religion'. We are to show tolerance of religion because we see 'man carried about, like an obstinate child in the arms of its mother, by what God has determined and done for his salvation in spite of his own opposition' (p. 299). Yet the very use of the word 'tolerance' in this context suggests that the theologian has an assured standing ground in relation to religion which is denied to other sinful men. There is a hint of patronage in Barth's language here which, on his own showing, is an indication that he is being led astray. The theologian is here speaking like the Pope.

Surely, one of the first things which the recognition of 'religion as the affair of godless man' should do is to make the Christian aware of his solidarity with other religious men. This in its turn should make him ready to listen, not with mere tolerance but with respect, to what men of other faiths than his own have to say about their religious experience before he can dare to make any observations about how it might be related to the revelation he has known in Christ. This in no way detracts from the finality of that revelation. On the contrary, as Barth himself has helped us to see so clearly in other contexts, it is this alone which shows a proper understanding of what that finality implies. For that finality cannot, in its nature, be an assumption from which the theologian can confidently start, as though he had such complete possession of Christian revelation that he knew beforehand exactly how God is likely to be related to every human situation. The finality of the Christian revelation can only be apprehended in faith. Otherwise, the strictures which Arnold Toynbee and others make against its exclusiveness are decisive. All religion, including the Christian religion, is the affair of godless man unless it is judged and renewed by justifying faith. This means that no one can distinguish between faith and that which is not faith, on his own part or on the part of his neighbour, until he has genuinely moved in alongside his neighbour with the humility of Christ and striven with him to perform the act of obedience which God seems to demand in that situation. We all have to make specific judgments about our own faith, and sometimes about that of our neighbour also, but they are judgments which must be qualified at every turn by the knowledge that it is God alone who is the final judge. This will ensure that our judgments are provisional, self-critical and informed at all times by charity. This means that they cannot be made without identification with our neighbour in his situation.

To recognize the godlessness in one's own religion is necessary in order to achieve true faith. It is this which the revelation of God in Christ enables sinful men to do. But to go on to identify that revelation with the religion of Christians or with the judgments of theologians is to fall into the very trap against which Barth himself has so eloquently warned us. Yet this is bound to happen when theologians take it upon themselves to prejudge the issue between other men in their religion and God, without first accepting the necessity to stand alongside them in their religious situation.[1]

Barth's negative attitude towards religion prevents him also from indicating the full extent of the dilemma confronting the man of faith in relation to religion. As he

---

[1] The practical consequences of this for the relation of Christian and non-Christian religions are obviously very great. What, for example, is the Reformed churchman to say to those Yodoist Buddhists mentioned by Barth after they have had it pointed out to them that the similarities between their faith and that of the Reformation cannot be of decisive significance? Must we simply conclude that any resemblances between them are purely coincidental and leave the matter at that?

himself insists, genuine faith issues in religion. There is a
true Christian religion. The more fully alive faith is, the
more it is honoured and blessed by God, the more richly
and vigorously it produces a heritage of religion with which
those who inherit it have to come to terms. This fact shows
how misleading it is to regard religion as the affair of godless man alone. If that were so, the situation would be
simpler. The dilemma becomes most acute when it is seen
that religion is also so much the affair of the godly man.
The 'rich man' of whom Jesus speaks is not only the man
who has many material possessions; he is pre-eminently the
religious man, who has been blessed with spiritual abund-
ance as God's righteous servant. It is this which makes so
scandalous to the disciples the idea that the rich man should
find it peculiarly difficult to enter the kingdom.

These qualifications must be made before we can accept
Barth's statements that religion is the enemy of faith and
that faith means the abolition of religion. Yet they serve
only to underline the truth of his main contention. Man's religion provides him with the final and most closely guarded
citadel in which he can defend himself against the divine
grace. Religion fulfils the positive function of making man
aware of the inadequacy of his own resources and ready to
lift up his eyes towards God, but of itself it cannot save
man. Faith working through love which transcends religion
and yet produces more religion and transcends religion once
more is alone that which justifies men in God's sight.

2. *Bonhoeffer on the End of Religion*

Qualifications which are not dissimilar have to be made
also of Bonhoeffer's treatment of religion as he has left it to
us in the tantalizingly brief observations which he made in
his letters from prison. His main contention is a triumphant
assertion of the way in which faith works through love to

release the Christian for action in freedom in the real world. The man of faith is released from self-preoccupation on the religious as well as on other levels, for identification with his neighbour in the day to day affairs of the world as the place in which he knows God and enjoys life. Like Kierkegaard's knight of faith, he 'realizes the universal human'. Bonhoeffer does not say this, but we can readily believe from the whole tenor of his teaching that he would have wanted to go on—in the way Kierkegaard did not—to define the Church, the *communio sanctorum*, as the company of those who, in communion with God in Christ, 'realize the universal human' and are set free for the true service of their fellows. It is religionless Christianity in this sense which truly bears fruit in holy worldliness.

Yet even here we are left uneasily wondering whether the point has been adequately stated because, perhaps under the direct influence of Barth, Bonhoeffer is working with an unduly negative interpretation of religion. Dr Eberhard Bethge, to whom many of the letters from prison were written, has now attempted to define four characteristics of religion in Bonhoeffer's view.[1]

First, it is individualistic. The religious man is preoccupied with himself and his interior states in such a way as to forget his neighbour, even though this individualism may take ascetic and apparently self-sacrificial forms. Secondly, it is metaphysical. God is brought in to complete, as the supernatural, a fundamentally man-centred view of reality. Thirdly, the religious interest becomes more and more one department of life only. Scientific discovery and other forces push it more and more into insignificant areas of life. And fourthly, the God of religion is a *deus ex machina*, one who comes in from the outside to help his children when they are in trouble. He is not the One at the centre of life, who

[1] *The Chicago Theological Seminary Register, February* 1961.

controls and directs it and meets and sustains us in our
strength as well as our weakness.

If this is a faithful account of what Bonhoeffer meant by
religion, we have to say that religion indeed frequently takes
these forms and that he is right to say that in these forms
it readily becomes corrupt and misleading and that we may
hope that the time for it is over. But we are still left with
these questions. Was there ever a right time for it, at least in
the Christian dispensation? And although the time for it
may be over, what hidden forces have been at work to make
possible a world where men are no longer likely to fall into
these 'religious traps' and what is their status? When we
are told that the world has now 'come of age' we assume
that this has not happened since, say, the eighteenth-century
Enlightenment or the rise of modern science but since Jesus
Christ has risen from the dead and poured out his Spirit
over mankind. The Enlightenment and the rise of science
are no more than expressions of this maturity in certain
realms of life. They may affect the way in which the man
of faith exercises his responsibility in the world but in themselves they do not do away with the necessity for religion,
if only because they themselves can become the agencies
which can foster new religion, as was very clear in the case
of the Enlightenment. The world's 'coming of age' does not
abolish religion. Both sin and faith will conspire to generate
more religion out of this mature world and the man of faith
will have to continue to vindicate his maturity in the only
way which has always been possible, by renewed faith working through love.

It is this which makes somewhat unconvincing Bonhoeffer's speculation—and in fairness to him it should be
recognized that it was not more than that—that we are moving into a religionless period in Western history and that, for
example, the irreligious working man must be reached in

other than religious ways. Many people who have been
'through religion', who have been over-dominated by the
'religious assumption', may very well be prepared to accept
Christian faith with a modicum of religious trappings. We
may think of educated persons from the East, for example,
who have rejected their Eastern religions and cannot accept
the Westernized life of the churches. Or we may consider
the children of pious Christian homes who have suffered
from over-exposure to religion. But even these will not
strictly be able to accept a 'religionless Christianity'. They
will be severe Puritans in relation to religion, and this indeed
may be a necessary and excellent thing. But the characteristic of the 'irreligious working man', in so far as it is possible to generalize about people of widely differing types,
is that he has been the victim of false ideology or has failed
to penetrate to the religious dimension. His situation is not
that he has achieved maturity but that he lives in a situation
in which maturity is required of him but where he refuses
to rise to the height of his calling. He is sinking back into
becoming one of the masses, whose characteristic is not
'religionlessness' but superficiality. A modern form of
'Methodism', of which Bonhoeffer disapproves, may yet
prove to be as successful in calling him out of the masses
for responsible personal existence as the old Methodism was
in the eighteenth and nineteenth centuries. Indeed, perhaps
the chief difference between the working men of Britain and
the USA and those of Continental Europe is that the former
have been exposed to more and better 'Methodism' under
various labels than the latter.

The same validity and similar qualifications attach to
Bonhoeffer's conception of the secret discipline by which the
man of faith lives in the world. The Christian community
needs to see more urgently today than ever before that it
expresses its obedience, and commends its faith, not by dis-

plays of personal or corporate piety nor by enunciating a Christian world-view—there can be more sophisticated versions of this than the MRA 'ideology' but their effect is not very different—but by its humble service of the world in the light of Christ. Our lights are to shine before men, but in such a way that it is our works and not ourselves that they see and so that they glorify with us God, our common father in heaven. The Christian betrays his calling if he parades before men the inner life which sustains these works, in the hope that men might be impressed and converted. It is more important than ever that the knight of faith look like an inspector of taxes, or like any other ordinary person going faithfully about his daily business.

This is true and needs saying in these days when the Christian community is disposed to overstrain itself with apparent evangelistic zeal, as though the truth of faith depended on its powers of religious salesmanship. Yet it also needs to be borne in mind that the secret discipline is not a private or an individual one. To make it that would, on Bonhoeffer's own showing, place it firmly back within the realm of religion. It is a discipline shared by the believer with his fellow-members of Christ, with whom he walks together in church order. The discipline is secret but it is also that of the fellowship of the mystery, the open secret of the Gospel. This forbids self-display and constantly reminds believers that they walk by faith and not by sight. It reminds them at every turn of the perils of religion. Yet it is a rich and joyful discipline also, in which people discover one another and the possibilities of life together in the world.[1]

Bonhoeffer's experience in prison was that he often found it easier to deal with apparently non-religious people than

[1] Bonhoeffer would be the last to deny this. See his early work *Sanctorum Communio* (Eng. trans., 1962, Collins), and his *Life Together* (Eng. trans., 1954, SCM Press and Harper, NY).

with the self-consciously pious. The experience has been
that of many other people in our own time. It is a reminder
of the unreality of the world into which a false preoccupation with religion can lead people; and it is a reminder also
of how faith releases people for true human community
life with all men, whether they bear a Christian label or not.
It does not, however, affect the fact that a degree of give-
and-take is possible in the communion of believers which is
rarely achieved even in the most genial contacts with those
who do not make a Christian profession. It may well be
that there is a dimension of meaning in Bonhoeffer's thought
to which we have failed to penetrate, but it is hard to resist
the conclusion that his plea for a 'religionless Christianity'
in this context means primarily a plea for re-definition of
the Church, of faith and of the religion of faith. It starts
from a fresh insight into the nature of Christian maturity as
freedom to serve with Christ in the real life of the world,
and it seeks to abolish much which passes for 'the life of the
Church' but which, in its tired flabbiness, is no more than a
quasi-religious conformity to this world which passes away.
It may well be a reminder also that those whose spiritual
roots are deep, as those of Bonhoeffer were by the time when
he worked for the anti-Nazi Resistance, may need less
formal religion for their day-to-day sustenance than most
professional practitioners of religion are eager to provide.

3. *The Pilgrim Church: Through Religion to Love*

Religion in the sense of the search for God and the response to God is inescapable. To be rich in religion, provided the religion is good, is also a mark of the divine
favour, as it was in Israel. Yet this becomes true only in
so far as we give heed to what both Barth and Bonhoeffer
in their slightly different ways say about religion as faith's
greatest enemy. Apart from God's grace, it certainly be-

comes a way of counting it 'something to be snatched at to be on an equality with God' and of 'glorying' in the sense Paul repudiates, failing to see that the preaching of Christ crucified means the divine judgment on even the finest of one's religious achievements. In such a situation, attention is deflected from God and from discerning his will and showing gratitude to him. It is given instead to preoccupation with oneself or with one's neighbour's religious estimate of oneself. That such self-centredness can find expression more readily through religious channels than in any other way is demonstrated by Jesus himself, both in his experience in dealing with the religious leaders of the Jews which led directly to the crucifixion and through his explicit teaching. The publican goes down to his house justified rather than the Pharisee not because he has a superior religious status to the Pharisee, who is the professionally religious man, but because the Pharisee has become so intoxicated with his religious wealth and so preoccupied with justifying himself in his use of it that he has failed to achieve the true self-transcendence of faith. The Pharisee is religious but the publican is penitent and it is through his penitence that the publican finds justification.

While Barth may be speaking of only one side of the truth when he says that the history of Christianity can be read as the history of the catastrophes which Christianity creates for itself, there is no doubt that the history provides us with plenty of such calamities. These arise not only in periods of corruption and glaring abuse but also in periods of renewal and reformation, or at least very shortly after such periods. Indeed, it frequently seems to happen that the more genuine the renewal is and the more successful the attempt to achieve a reformation, the greater the danger becomes of making religion an end in itself and not the servant of the will of God. People have made determined efforts to find 'true religion' by establishing an effective discipline in church life, or by gathering together a community of those who will profess that they have been consciously called by God to walk together in close fellowship, or by ensuring that pure doctrine is adequately defined and taught, or by maintaining an elaborate system of sacramental devotion, or by following a particular method of seeking the Spirit's guidance, or by faithfulness to what they conceive to be the Bible and the Bible alone. No one has any right to say that these efforts have failed. Faith finds expression in different ways in different situations. What can be confidently stated is that none of these methods has guaranteed or can guarantee success. It is the characteristic temptation of the second generation in the succession of those who made the original effort to assume that they do, with the result that they turn them into 'an affair of godless man'. No effort at reformation can be definitive and complete. Reformation must be a perennial activity and must constantly take new forms because man is always trying to seize the glory from God and because God's lordship has to be re-asserted in the changing circumstances of life.

What then can be done to ensure that religion is that true religion which is fulfilled in fresh acts of faith issuing in love? It is at this point, in the light of our discussion of Barth and Bonhoeffer, that we can profitably look at the experience of the men of the New Testament and, in particular, at the experience of the man who might almost be taken as the archetype of the religious man, the apostle Paul.

Paul is the heir of the full riches of the religious tradition of Israel, 'circumcised the eighth day, of the stock of Israel, of the tribe of Benjamin, a Hebrew of the Hebrews, as touching the Law a Pharisee' (Phil. 3.5). And he is religious not only according to the manner of the old Israel but also

according to that of the new. He has suffered with his Lord
and known those ecstatic experiences which are given only
to those who hold close communion with their Lord (II Cor.
11.23-29; 12.1-4). All these, on the ordinary human level,
might give legitimate cause for glorying. They are good
things, signs of the divine favour. But they cease to be good
if they make Paul forget the real source of his strength,
which is in his Lord and not in himself. He glories, therefore, in his weaknesses which drive him to a greater awareness of his dependence on his Lord, for it is when he is made
to see his weakness that, through the Lord, he is made strong
(II Cor. 12.10).

Paul says this, not through any perversity or delight in
paradox, but because he knows so clearly that the inter-
action of God's grace and man's sin means that the Christian life is always one of tension between acceptance and
rejection, joy and sorrow, death and life (II Cor. 4.7-11). If
the exceeding greatness of the power is truly to be of God,
we must never forget that we have the treasure of God's
grace in earthen vessels, even though they may be very
religious vessels. We are justified by faith and not by works,
and in Paul's case it is made very clear that works include
religious works. And lest anyone should imagine that these
are, after all, only the theological subtleties of a man of
genius, which need not unduly trouble the ordinary believer,
the most direct and comprehensive statement of the very
same point is to be found in the hymn in praise of love in
I Cor. 13.

It is, perhaps, also worth saying that this is not to be
regarded simply as Paulinism, which must be duly balanced
by other emphases of the New Testament. Love and faith
are defined in a sharper and more precise way in Paul than
in John, but the closely argued and passionate debates between Jesus and the Jews in the Fourth Gospel show that

the issue between religion and faith arose no less radically for John. Paul is not necessarily more 'Barthian' than the rest of the New Testament, but he does write more self-consciously as a theologian, against the background of the religion of Israel and very definitely in fulfilment of the prophetic tradition. It is this which makes his experience peculiarly illuminating to the Church at all periods of her history in trying to deal with the relation between religion and faith.

To place the prophetic strain in the Bible in opposition to the priestly is to create a false antithesis. The Church can learn a great deal about herself from ideas in the New Testament which arose out of the cultus in Israel and false prophets can arise at least as easily as false priests. Both the prophetic and the priestly elements in Israel find their fulfilment in Jesus Christ. Throughout her history, however, the Church has shown a greater readiness to succumb to the distinctive temptations of priesthood than to those of prophecy. She has always found it easy to slip into becoming an extremely rigid institution administered by the members of a priestly caste who conceive of their function in ever more prescribed and formalized ways and who encourage prophetic protests, if they do so at all, only within the limits which they have carefully set. The Holy Spirit keeps the Church moving toward the fulfilment of the divine purpose and, while true prophecy cannot exist without true priesthood, the Spirit speaks chiefly through prophecy because the Church is always in danger of settling down where she is and trying to domesticate the Spirit according to her own ideas. This is the characteristic ecclesiastical way of becoming conformed to this world which passes away, of becoming secularized without holiness behind the masks of holiness. To give no opportunity for the Spirit of prophecy to express itself in the Church, or to limit its range, is to estab-

lish the reign of men rather than of God in the Church.
The question of how religion can be true religion, which
is kept in the way of faith, is the chief question lying behind
all discussions of church order, and they are likely to prove
superficial if this is not clearly seen. Church order is not
only a matter of church organization and administration,
although it is certainly these also, but also one of the shape
which the Church's life has in the world as it seeks to be
conformed to the divine purpose. When it is understood in
this sense, it becomes clear that it is only through justification by faith and following the 'Protestant principle' that
church order can be properly evaluated.

It is essential that the *relativity* of all religious observances be frankly accepted. They are strictly relative to the
worship and praise of God, to the discovery of his will and
to the fulfilment of that will in action. Now here it is important to safeguard ourselves from a whole host of misunderstandings which are ready to rush in to becloud the issue
and conceal it from us. We are not implying that true worship cannot be an end in itself, only that religious observances, even the most pious and exalted, do not become true
worship simply by taking place. Nor are we implying that
worship cannot itself be an event in the spiritual realm
which may have far-reaching practical consequences. On
the contrary, what we are concerned about is that that event
should be defined, and its practical consequences actively
sought.

It is, of course, right to think of religious observances as
ways through which it is possible to come to know and to
enjoy God, under the conditions of earthly life, which are
foretastes of the way in which he will be known and enjoyed
for ever. It is also right to insist that if men become too
anxious to assert that all worship should have a directly
edificatory purpose, as the Puritans were disposed to do,

some of its richness and spontaneity is lost. We cordially acknowledge the important measure of truth in Von Hügel's well-known dictum that religion is an 'is-ness' as well as an 'ought-ness'. Yet it must still be maintained that all religious observances, even the most solemn, are human actions and partake to the full of the ambiguity of human actions. They are not the only actions required of those who strive to be obedient to God. This may seem to be the most obvious of remarks to make, yet it must be seen that to make religious observances and activities bearing a religious label an end in themselves is one of the most persistent and insidious of temptations. The due performance of the appropriate rituals, or the establishment and maintenance of a flourishing institution with the conventional round of activities which come to be expected of churches, quickly absorbs all the energies of the religious life. And they no less quickly gather around themselves elaborate vested interests which are reinforced by the amazingly powerful drive of religious institutions towards conservative defensiveness once their vitality begins to diminish.

The *securitas*—in Luther's sense of spiritual complacency, contrasted with *certitudo* or the proper assurance given in faith—encouraged by this attitude is undoubtedly one of the greatest enemies of true faith, and churches can have no hope of overcoming it unless they are acutely aware of it and are ceaselessly in vigilance against it. They must always remember that they are pilgrim churches, that their home is not here and that they are set in the right way only as they keep moving towards that home. So far is true eschatological expectation from making churches indifferent to their task in the world that it is the only force strong enough to prevent them from settling down to self-admiration and to keep them open and flexible to the promptings of the Spirit. Without this goal, they cease to strive.

It follows from this that the Church's earthly form is not related to her true purpose unless it expresses her existence as a pilgrim Church. The Church has an earthly form. She is a visible community. But her form is that of a community *in via*. Church order is not a system of arrangements for making the temporary camps of the people of God as convenient and manageable and dignified as possible; it is more like a system of travel arrangements, with special devices for coping with constant emergencies and for ensuring that stragglers are kept on the move. Whenever the Church meets her Lord in his Word, it always involves a fresh encounter with him and a fresh venture of faith which means casting off earthly *securitas*. The sacraments are also meant to be understood in the same way. Baptism testifies to death and resurrection, the decisive break between the old man and the new, as the first principle of the Church's life. The Lord's Supper both reassures the Lord's people of his continuing presence with them in the midst of a world which passes away, and reminds them that they do not know him now as they will know him hereafter. This should prompt them to look the more eagerly for the signs of his appearing. The common life of the Church should be open and flexible, severely functional and readily adaptable, strongly disciplined and yet capable of the spontaneity which comes with maturity, like that of a seasoned army on the march through disputed territory where enemies constantly lurk but over which their King's sway is being steadily reasserted.

This dynamic conception of church order is not, as its critics allege, individualistic and anarchic. It would be so were it not for the presence of the Holy Spirit, with the Spirit's unifying and reconciling power and with the Spirit's gifts which lead the Church to maturity in freedom. It is undeniable, however, that it confronts most of the church orders in Christendom with a severe challenge. These are predominantly conservative and defensive in character, almost essentially so in Catholicism and very similar in practice, if not always in theory, in Protestantism. The result is that the Spirit seems to call the people of God forward almost as often in despite of the official spokesmen of the churches as through their agency. Even when all allowance is made for the fact that churches have to show a proper concern for secular continuity and institutional stability, it has to be acknowledged that history indicates that, to put it at its mildest, justifying faith which is blessed by the Spirit cannot be identified with the religion of the churches. This is not to say that the churches are not essential if faith is to find expression in terms of life on this earth, but it is to qualify radically many of the pretensions which churches make for themselves. Faith moves through religion beyond religion into the venture of obedience which expresses itself in love. The mark of a good church order is not the ease with which its clergy can keep their people in control but the extent of its ability to keep thrusting the church's religion into the crisis of faith and to keep doing this even while it is surrounded by all the precious fruits of faith. What this means in more specific terms for the life of churches today will be the theme of our fourth and fifth chapters.

Another way in which churches can strive to ensure that their religion becomes the true religion of faith is one which is available, and necessary, in every situation. They should strive to be *penitent* churches, who maintain a habit of vigilant self-criticism. This self-criticism should range over every part of the Church's life, but it will clearly be no more than a habit of anxious introspection unless it uses adequate standards of criticism. It is a primary responsibility of the ministry of the Word and the sacraments to remind the Church of these criteria. It is part of the function of theological study to define these criteria with reference to the constantly changing circumstances in which the Church lives. When it does this, theology can become the intellectual expression of the Church's repentance in relation to the saving events of the Gospel itself and it can point the way to the form which repentance should take in the relationships of daily life.

No one with even the slightest acquaintance with the history of theology would want to claim that a tradition of vigorous theological work provides a very strong guarantee that a church will always succeed in thrusting beyond religion into faith. The reverse seems often to be the case. Theology can easily become ideological, doing little more than to supply arguments by which churches can display envy, malice and all uncharitableness towards their neighbours and do so with a good conscience. It also can become an end in itself, like religious observance, leading its practitioners to believe that a satisfactory theological formulation is a substitute for, and not simply a preliminary to, action in obedience. 'Theologism' may not be a very strong temptation among English-speaking churchmen, but among the more theologically-gifted German-speaking churchmen it is more powerful.

All this is so notorious that it is easy to become cynical at the very idea of theology's being able to act effectively as the servant of the Church's service. But to press such an attitude to its logical conclusion is to despair of the Gospel, for it is equivalent to saying that it is useless to suppose that the word which is spoken in the Church's proclamation can ever truly become the Word of God. The history of theology, despite all its failures, does not bear this out. Theology has been a reconciling and renewing as well as a divisive or reactionary influence in the life of the Church. It is not an accident that periods of creative theological statement, as distinct from elaborate theological systematization, have often been periods of vigorous revival. In our own time, one of the chief impulses lying behind the movement of renewal and reformation we call the Ecumenical Movement has been a critical theological rediscovery of neglected elements in the Bible and in the doctrine of the Church. Theology is certainly no panacea, but if it is good theology—which means, among other things, that it is pursued with a clear eye upon its own limitations—it is an essential instrument for enabling the ministry to fulfil its critical and prophetic function. For a true theological understanding will always lead the Church to see that faith works supremely through love, through identification with our neighbour in the life of the world in the setting of God's purpose. It will insist that the Church remains at the level of religion, no matter how prophetic and full of insight and ready to commit itself it may be, unless it strives always to follow 'the more excellent way' of love.

This is the true 'holy worldliness', identification with Christ in love of our neighbour. The faith of the Reformation has suffered from grave distortion and abuse, and has been prevented from spreading through Christendom as it should have done, because it has never been emphasized with sufficient imagination and power by the Reformed churches that the hymn to love in I Cor. 13 is solidly of a piece with the exposition of justification by faith in Rom. 3-7. Not only are they by the same author, they are speaking about the same reality under different aspects. The gifts of which I Cor. 12 speaks are the fruit of faith, and we may properly think of them as the expression of religion. We are indeed, as Paul says, to 'cultivate the best gifts'. It is ingratitude to God to do otherwise. Yet without love, they and the whole Christian religion in all its splendour stand under the same judgment as all other human activity.

In the chapter which precedes the discussion of spiritual gifts and the hymn in praise of love, Paul says that to receive the Lord's Supper unworthily is to eat and drink damnation to oneself. In this, the Lord's Supper must be taken as the type of all religious activity. For to receive the Supper unworthily means primarily to do so in a way which leaves one preoccupied with oneself and not released for God and for one's neighbour. Faith is the recovery of our proper manhood, of our maturity. We 'come of age' and find our freedom from the bondage of false gods to hold communion in love with each other. Faith is 'the realization of the universal human' which enables us to 'deal truly with one another in love'. We do not claim that this is anything more or less than the unchanging heart of the Christian gospel. What we do claim is that the notions of 'religionless Christianity' and 'holy worldliness' help us to recover, as we always need to recover, the gospel's authentic freshness and power.

III

The God Above God

WE have seen that the idea of 'the God above God' is one which has an appeal in these days for those who are deeply concerned with ultimate meanings but find themselves unimpressed with the way in which the spokesmen of the Christian community speak about God and witness to his reality in their actions. The idea has received currency chiefly through some references to a 'God above God' in Paul Tillich's *The Courage To Be*.[1] But, like Bonhoeffer's references to 'religionless Christianity', these pages are brief and sketchy, and tantalize almost as much as they illuminate.

1. *The Hidden God*

Like some of Tillich's other ideas, this one comes very near, in the way in which he expresses it, to ideas which have been denounced by the churches at various stages of their history as dangerous heresy. The Gnostics spoke, in effect, of a god, or of several gods, beyond God as revealed in Christ, and mysticism has often been fascinated by the beyond in God. Yet the real root of the idea lies much more deeply in the soil of Christian history than Tillich has yet suggested and, provided it is carefully defined and safeguarded against obvious misunderstandings, it can be of the greatest assistance to the Church in trying to discern the will of God today. Its affinity with the ideas lying behind religionless Christianity and holy worldliness can be shown to be very close.

[1] 1952 (Nisbet and Yale), pp. 182-90.

The root of this idea lies in that of the hiddenness of God. Paul expressed something of it in his discussion of the mystery of the divine election, chiefly in Rom. 9-11. Augustine and Anselm, in their different ways, were acutely aware of it. Luther developed it, in relation to his idea of the *deus absconditus,* with great imaginative power. And it has received sober and very constructive and original re-statement by Karl Barth.[1] Barth emphasizes that belief in the hiddenness of God does not arise from human incapacity but from the divine perfection. It is because God is holy, sovereign and transcendent and retains the initiative in dealing with men that we speak of him as the hidden God. Our awareness of him as hidden is involved with the very fact of revelation. He is not self-evident; he has to make himself known. And he makes himself known as the One who is the Lord, out of no human necessity but because of his love.

Now this is far from an attempt to labour an obvious point because, unless we start from this awareness of God as hidden in his revelation, we do not have the right attitude towards God. Our attitude towards him is one of 'sight' and not of faith, and while we remain sinners that must mean that we have the initiative over against God and, therefore, deny his lordship. As Barth himself puts it in a cumbersome but very significant sentence, 'It is most important to establish all this expressly, because it follows inevitably that if the inner limitation which divides and separates our viewing, thinking and speaking as such from the being of God is overlooked or forgotten or denied, and if this happens in responsibility towards God's revelation, the external limitation is also lost, as is the character of the revelation of God as the source and norm of our speech about God, and the

[1] See his chapter on the 'Hiddenness of God' in *Church Dogmatics,* vol. ii. 1, pp. 179-204.

unconditional subordination of the latter to this source and norm' (p. 195). And as he goes on to say, what then happens is that 'our cognition ceases to be the mirror of God's revelation and God's revelation begins to be the mirror of our cognition' (p. 196).

The venture of true faith becomes unnecessary in such circumstances because man remains in control. Men do not need to knock and seek and find before they know God and learn his will because he is an object constantly before their eyes. But God, the hidden God, remains the Lord even in his revelation, and when men know him he is not given over completely into their hands, to be used as they think fit. Their knowledge is real knowledge; God truly enters into communion with his children. Yet he does not cease to be the Lord. That is why the result of asking, seeking and knocking is not simply finding, but the kind of finding which prompts men to go on asking, seeking and knocking. To put the matter in a different way, the Holy Spirit does dwell with the people of God but as their leader, their judge and their guide, a pillar of cloud by day and of fire by night, and not as a reality which is to be discovered only by looking at the past history and the present reality of the Church's own life.

2. *Doubt and Faith*

It follows from this that behind every idea of God and of his will which presents itself and commends itself as true to the Church there begins to form another idea which commends itself as more true in the new situation into which faithfulness to the original vision has led the Church. This happens both because, in a sinful world where everything passes away into nothingness, even our words and the images they convey are subject to wastage and distortion, and because God is a personal reality who reveals himself in fresh encounters with his children in the ever-changing circumstances of life.

To take the more negative aspect of this first, our ideas about God may be sufficiently true and adequately expressed in a particular situation to give us the conviction that we are in communion with him and can learn his will. Events may 'prove' to us that this is so, because God appears to honour our faith. But it is vital that we should not assume from this that the formulation we have achieved is definitive, and need no longer require critical re-examination. For it is quite certain that, however satisfactory our formulation, it contained within it elements of error and distortion, which may not at the time of the formulation have been sufficient to lead us astray but which become increasingly evident as we move into a new situation. No longer corresponding to the realities of men's relation with God, these words become barriers to, rather than means of, communion with God. This does not mean that a fresh set of words have to be created by each generation of theologians. There are certain words, as there are certain images, which have a normative character, namely, those of Scripture and, in a lesser degree, those of the Creeds and Confessions which try to concentrate on the permanent rather than the transitory aspects of God's revelation to men. It does mean, however, that no words and no images can be taken for granted without constant re-examination. That includes the words of Scripture, Creeds and Confessions, although, in varying degree, these impose an obligation on all future generations of Christians to understand and appreciate them before they proceed to a formulation of their own. The critical work of theology must go on unremittingly. To put it on a more practical level still, preaching Sunday by Sunday must be the fruit of a genuinely fresh and living encounter between God and the Church. Otherwise, the Church's orthdoxy ceases to be the right way of glorifying God and becomes a prison in which she tries to entrap the living Spirit.

On the more positive side, God is personal and has a continuing personal relation to his children. Even if he prefers to speak the language of Zion, he does not say exactly the same thing to all his children all the time. The Lord hath yet more light and truth to break forth from his Word, as he must if he is the living God who has a purpose for his people which he is ceaselessly directing to its fulfilment. This means that he must be waited upon in prayer, meditation and hard thought, by the Church corporately as well as by the individual, and wrestled with until he reveals his name anew. When he does so, the Church will find herself thrust into new situations, where none of the old landmarks exist to guide her and where she can no longer proceed on the basis of precedent, where, in fact, she can do no other than commit herself in faith to her Lord.

If it be protested, as it will be, that this exposes the Church to the danger of being led astray by those who mistake their own spirit for the Spirit of God, we may agree but point out that this danger is inescapable for those who seek to live by the Spirit. It needs to be said also that the dangers to which the 'Spiritualizers' succumb are not greater than those into which those fall who, in their conservative anxiety to guard the deposit of faith at all costs, do no more than bury their talent in the ground. The fact that the latter temptation is the one to which, throughout their history, most parts of the Church have been particularly vulnerable —to such an extent that some of them have come to regard it as a virtue—does not make it any the less culpable or the less deadly. Our Lord certainly promises us that the Holy Spirit will dwell within the Church, but only on condition that the Church will follow the leading of the Spirit. If a

Church refuses to try to keep up with the Spirit and prefers to live in the fourth or the thirteenth or the sixteenth or the nineteenth century, or even in its own version of the first century or in the twenties or thirties of the twentieth century, experience shows that the Spirit seeks more effective instruments for its purpose. That Church, whatever label it may bear, is no longer in the place where the Spirit dwells and leads. The Spirit insists upon living in the present moment, in the now in which salvation is always declared, and it always calls the people of God forward in the light of the ultimate purpose of God revealed decisively in the cross, resurrection and exaltation of Jesus Christ.

The fact that the ideas of God possessed by men—which must, of course, be distinguished from God himself—have to be subjected to constant review, and that God himself invites his children to press forward to a clearer notion of him, throws light on the relation between faith and doubt. That relation is always complicated.

Doubt concerning the reality of God arises only because we are sinful men who live in a sinful world, for to cast doubt on God is a form of rebellion against him. Yet there is another sense in which it has to be said that genuine faith can only exist if it is found in close connection with a form of doubt and that the presence of an actively doubting spirit is an index of the possibility of living faith being reached. We have been at pains to insist that faith does not exist in a vacuum or in a pious half-world of religion but in the midst of the world which passes away. This means that it is to be found always in the presence of its contradiction. It has to overcome that which stands in its way and denies that God is God. What this opposition is will vary with the experience of each individual or community and it will vary also at different times or with different levels of experience of the same individual or community. The contradiction of

faith may come in the form of a specific temptation to perform a selfish or cruel action which contradicts the reality
of a God who is love. On the intellectual level, it will come
in the form of facts or experiences which present a challenge because it does not seem possible to make them ration-
ally coherent with the reality of God. More radically, it will
sometimes come in the form of a temptation to despair of
all meaning and to surrender to chaos. Luther knew this
temptation very powerfully, and it is this which Tillich has
in mind when he speaks, in his curiously abstract way, of
faith as 'the courage to be'. But come in one form or another it will, and if faith is to be a reality it will have to be
unremittingly faced.

It is of the essence of the Christian Gospel that it must
be accepted as the truth, and as the truth in the sense of the
Fourth Gospel—the reality in which men have their being.
Men cannot live, therefore, with something which appears
to be a contradiction of the Gospel without striving to re-
solve that contradiction. To pretend that the contradiction
is not there, out of a misplaced piety, is to deny the Christian claim to be the truth and to accept it surreptitiously as
a form of unreality. In this sense, it can be said that to refuse to face doubt and acknowledge it for what it is, is itself
the most defiant form of unbelief. Theology itself implies
doubt and lacks all reality without it. Theological reflection
is not a retreat from the world into a different realm from
this, one of timeless truth where the voice of doubt is stilled
and where God is contemplated in the purity of his being.
It is an act of overcoming the world in encounter on the intellectual level, at the place where the world is struggling
most fiercely, in the realm of religion nearest to faith. And
in the struggle it uses the perishable, mutable, imperfect
images and words of the world. So far is theological reflection from being unworldly that it could be argued that the

nature of the world stands most clearly revealed the more closely it comes to the light of God in his revelation. This is why Kierkegaard's famous question 'Can a theologian be saved?' is far from being a merely rhetorical one.

It is, incidentally, his failure to face the implications of this fact that makes Tillich draw far too sharp a distinction between dogmatic and apologetic theology in trying to justify the method he adopts in his *Systematic Theology*.[1] Faith has to wrestle with its contradiction the more sharply the nearer it gets to the heart of revelation. It is an intolerably superficial conception of revelation, one which misunderstands what the cross and resurrection of Christ have to say about God and about the human situation, which can assume that the voice of doubt is stilled when we examine what the Bible says but that it is active when we consider the relation between faith and the 'questions of modern man'. It is not surprising that Tillich never says precisely who this modern man is, or what makes his questions so particularly authoritative, or why they should be different in kind from the questions posed by ancient man, or what their relation is to the questions posed by God to man in his self-revelation. There may be justification for making some kind of distinction between dogmatic and apologetic theology, although this is arguable, but it is a distinction on a strictly secondary level. Otherwise, Tillich's 'God above God' can quickly cease to be the hidden God revealed in Christ who retains his freedom in the revelation; it can become no more than the name given by the theologian to the vitality produced by his own interest in his subject, an interest which remains merely aesthetic even when it contem-

[1] 1953 (Nisbet and Chicago), vol. i, pp. 6-8. By dogmatic theology we take him to mean the systematic exposition of the Christian faith by the Church in its own traditional terms, and by apologetic theology, its systematic exposition in response to the questions about life and destiny posed by the men of a particular generation.

plates the very abyss of meaninglessness. Tillich's theology operates on too profound a level for him to fall into this danger himself, but its failure to lead men directly to confrontation with the revelation of the living God as declared by the men of the Bible never finally lays the suspicion that this might, after all, be interpreted as no more than a very sophisticated form of religious humanism.

That faith has constantly to vindicate itself in the face of doubt, and has indeed often to seek out and develop doubt in order to do so, is the theologian's greatest safeguard against the peril of 'glorifying' in his religious achievements through theological work. It ensures that his theology is centred on the Cross, a *theologia crucis*. Not only does the theologian have to realize at every step of the way that he is at the same time righteous and sinful, *simul justus et peccator*; he will also be careful not to make excessive claims for his subject as against other subjects and not to assert his own views or those of his own school or denomination with too much self-confidence. Even though his is an enterprise shot though with sin, he will remember Luther's robust advice, *pecca fortiter,* and sin the more bravely, embarking upon it with a stout heart. But his hope will be in the promise of God and not in his own insight and authority. The fact that he has always to allow doubt to carry its full weight with him will help him to realize that this is indeed his situation and that it is through the grace of God alone that he can be the servant of the Church's service of God.

3. *Honest and Dishonest Doubt*

When the idea of the 'God above God' is interpreted in this way, it can be seen that it has far-reaching implications for the way in which we understand the finality of the Christian faith. In particular, it provides us with a new perspective in which to view the familiar disputes which rage between the orthodox and the heterodox or, to put it more accurately in this instance, between the defenders of established positions and those who give expression to doubts and difficulties about the truth of those established positions. In such situations, it is by no means clear that the way of faith is necessarily that which has come to be considered orthodox. To pursue doubts and difficulties certainly has its own perils also, and those who are unaware of them, or who find it possible to dramatize themselves while they pursue them, are certainly misled. But churchmen are nearly always more aware of these dangers than they are of the dangers of remaining in the same place. They do not allow sufficiently for the fact that to remain in the same place for a long time is a sure indication that one is not keeping up with the onward movement of the divine purpose. Those who give voice to doubts and difficulties may do so because they no longer abide in the truth and have been deceived by the devil, the father of lies. But they may also be doubters because a deeper faith in the reality of God than some of them may be able to express, or even be aware of, gives them courage to venture into the unknown without the comfort and re-assurance which an established position appears to give. Frequently they give the impression that it is this conviction of the finality of God, behind all appearances which deny him, that alone gives them strength honestly to state their doubts.

The experience of many of the great mid-Victorians who gave expression to their doubts concerning the Christian faith is particularly illuminating here. It is more illuminating than that of some of our latter-day doubters, whose difficulties may often appear to take a more violent and radical form, because the mid-Victorians give the impression of knowing much more what they are talking about. They had the advantage of a religious upbringing and, in some instances, of genuine religious experience. In the case of many of them, the Christian can truthfully say, as he considers them in the setting of their time, 'There, but for the grace of God, go I', whereas with many modern unbelievers his chief feeling is irritation at their complacency, ignorance and misunderstanding.

Take George Eliot for example. She speaks in one place of living without the Christian faith as being like living without opium. What exactly she meant by that it is not possible for us at this time to say and, fortunately, we are not required to decide, but to discuss what she might have meant helps us to see more clearly how the notion of a god beyond our ideas of God affects our attitude to the Christian faith. It could mean what George Eliot herself would probably have said it did mean, that she had become truly 'disenchanted'. The subtle magic of the Christian faith had lost its power and it had been exposed for the psychological trick it was. Now she could look out upon the world with cold realism, seeing things as they are, without illusion and without pretence. This is a painful experience, so painful that it is understandable if craving for the soothing warmth of the old addiction returns from time to time, but it is a bracing and stimulating one as well. New self-mastery and dignity are gained and the true way through life is more clearly seen. But in the light of all that followed, not only in George Eliot's own case but in that of many who came after her in the world of English thought and letters, a strong case could be made out for a very different version of what had actually taken place. It could be that the opium she was rejecting was not Christian faith itself but that narrow and already decaying version of Evangelicalism which was the operative form of Christianity in the circles in which she had grown up and which was proving itself inadequate to deal with the authentic new experiences with which a rapidly changing and expanding world was confronting its most alert children.[1] The difference between a scientific and a religious approach to reality presented people a hundred years ago with a sharper challenge and filled them with a far greater sense of venturing into dark unknown territory than it does today. In George Eliot's day, not only were all but a minority of churchmen showing a reluctance to make this venture but some of them were actively resisting those who did and trying to retreat into a simpler past. To repudiate such an attitude under the inescapable constraint of new truth may well have been the way of faith, even though it may have taken the form at the time of apparent hostility to some of the most cherished ideas of the religious community. The fact that some courageous souls did take that road and emerged with their faith all the more firm shows that this could easily have been. Whether this was so in the particular case of George Eliot is, of course, a matter for discussion. But the critic who understands what the notions of 'religionless Christianity' and the 'God above God' are trying to express will give more weight to the continuing moral maturity, insight and compassion of her work than to the heterodoxy of some of her opinions. The world she looked upon without the opium of Christian belief looks so much like what many others say they see as a result of that belief that it is hard to think that the Christianity she cast off was the real thing. Religion can undoubtedly become a very powerful opium, although it needs to be said against Marx that there have been few groups in history less addicted to it than the urbanized proletariat which he described. Faith, however, is essentially the rediscovery of truth and asks to be judged as such. It works by love, the char-

[1] It is this which Bertrand Russell still appears to think of when he speaks of Christianity. See his *Why I Am Not a Christian*, 1927 (Watts).

acteristic Christian quality, the fulfilment of human nature and the one which it is impossible to counterfeit.

In all this we may appear to be saying what another Victorian doubter, Tennyson, said in an oft-quoted phrase, that 'there lives more faith in honest doubt . . . than in half your creeds'. This, in its turn, may seem to be giving surprising aid and comfort to theological liberals, who have been among those who have quoted those words most often. If it gives any aid and comfort to the theological liberals, no one should begrudge it to them; they have had little enough offered to them recently. In so far as they have insisted upon the need for constant effort to lay hold on the reality of faith in the ever-changing circumstances of life, they have surely been in the right. They have been especially in the right when they have called attention to the fact that the present is a time of radical upheaval and change and that the adjustments of religious outlook needed within it must be expected to be great. It cannot be maintained that these adjustments have yet been made upon an adequate scale. The complaint against the theological liberals cannot be made on these grounds, but on the ground that they thought of the situation in which they found themselves in over-simple and over-confident terms. This can be demonstrated in many ways, but the only aspect which need concern us now is their attitude towards doubt. There may indeed be more faith in honest doubt than in half our creeds. The points which many liberals overlooked, especially those who have been liberal spokesmen for a long time and now possess a deeply-entrenched orthodoxy of their own, are those which Tennyson himself was careful to safeguard himself against. Honest doubt is not a commodity which it is easy to come by. It is, in fact, one of the rarest in the world. And Tennyson did not say 'all' but 'half' our creeds. That is to say, he was prepared to reckon with the possibility that there was truth in some of the creeds. This many latter-day liberals have not done, using the obvious and long-standing difficulties presented by the creeds and all the systems of orthodox theology as an excuse for not examining them to discover how much truth they contain and refusing to enter into constructive discussion with those who are attached to them.

Honest doubt is the underside of faith and to distinguish between honest and dishonest doubt is one of the primary functions of theology as a critical discipline. It is the theological aspect of that self-examination which leads to repentance. And the modern world is often an unfavourable environment for theological activity not because the 'questions posed by modern man' are necessarily of peculiar difficulty but because it is unusually full of dishonest doubt. There is the dishonesty of many people who have been scientifically trained or who have been deeply influenced by what they allege to be a scientific outlook, who prejudge the whole religious issue by saying that it has no right to exist in a tidy scientific picture of the universe. These people, under the guise of scientific objectivity, do no more than make a gesture of impatience in the face of the complexity of the human situation. Or there is the dishonesty of the discussion of religious matters by self-consciously literary intellectuals, where the chief concern of some of the participants appears to be not to reach the truth of these difficult matters but to project images of themselves as men of sensitive awareness, whose opinions on these matters reflect great credit on their own intelligence, critical acumen and gifts for literary expression. There is the dishonesty also of the self-consciously 'liberal' preacher, who is constantly drawing unfavourable contrasts between the men of the Old Testament and 'the ages of faith' on the one hand and his own enlightened congregation on the other, and who dramatizes himself as a man of exceptional courage because he refuses to make up his mind over matters which most Christians believe call inescapably for decision, celebrating eloquently Sunday by Sunday his ability to seek for but never to arrive at the truth.

But these are only overt forms of dishonest doubt. Most of us would have to admit to knowing much subtler forms of it in our own experience, whatever our professed beliefs. In these days, dishonest doubt is probably more pervasive than dishonest faith. Many of the difficulties concerning God's reality and power which we encounter today arise chiefly because of our reluctance honestly to face his claim upon our lives. We are too proud and think too highly of ourselves as special cases, or we are too attached to our family or class or nation or denomination to be prepared to commit ourselves to God. What frequently happens with many people today is particularly insidious because it comes so close to the attitude we are trying to commend: they become absorbed in worldly courses which may be good in themselves but which they come to love more than they love God—delight in the beauty of the natural world, enjoyment of the life of scholarship in the academic community, preoccupation with the day-to-day activities of business or of politics. They cease to see God's hand in these because they have stopped looking for it in case he should lead them in a way contrary to their inclinations. They are no longer in the place where his Spirit moves and they begin to wonder whether he really exists. This is dishonest doubt.

What are the tests of honest doubt? Two at least have been implicit in our argument so far. The first is that such doubt should be existential. This, it will be clear, does not mean that the doubter will necessarily be an 'existentialist', in the sense of belonging to a philosophical group who accept that name. It means that he will find himself genuinely engaged on the level of experience appropriate to the subject of his enquiry. In relation to God, of course, this means the most fundamental level of all. His doubt will not be honest unless he finds himself fighting for his life. Not all the judgments which men are required to make concerning the Christian faith are of this character. It is one of the vices of the champions of the various kinds of orthodoxy to try to surround many secondary judgments with the importance which belongs only to the primary one—in regard to questions of Biblical scholarship, for example. But the closer man comes to the heart of the encounter of faith, the more existential does his engagement become.

Another way of putting this same point is by saying that doubt concerning God's reality should press upon him the urgency of the question, 'How shall a man live?' The ethical question is inextricably involved with the metaphysical one. What made the doubt of some of the great Victorians suspect was their refusal to see this, and their confident assumption that the moral life would continue to stand in its own right even when the throne of the universe had been shown to be vacant. The question concerning God and the question concerning any validity or even meaning which our actions possess cannot be dissociated from one another. If we are able to treat the existence of God as a matter of speculative interest alone, our enquiry is not an honest one.

Yet this test is inadequate without the other. This is that the doubter must continue, in his doubt, to be sustained by a spirit of love. If it cannot be love directed positively towards the God whose existence is now called into question, it must at least be love towards the truth and it cannot be genuine love towards the truth unless it is also love towards his neighbour in the truth. This may seem to beg the whole question. Is not the whole point of doubt lost—or at least does it not lose its radical, its existential, character—unless the reality of love also is called into question? Yet here we do seem to come up against something in the human situation which we cannot get beyond. Doubt is dishonest unless it is disinterested, and disinterestedness cannot be achieved without love of the truth. And human nature is such that love of the truth seems impossible unless it carries with it love of the neighbour in the truth. Without that, it is a form of self-love, and self-love inevitably leads to that distortion of the truth in the interests of one's pride which is of the essence of dishonest doubt.

This apparent argument in a circle does not treat doubt with complacency. No one has the right to deny that honest doubt may lead a man to despair. A good deal of what we call despair may indeed be the fruit of an improper self-love, but human tragedy is such a reality that doubt which passes the tests we have described may yet lead, in some situations, to a conclusion where suicide seems to be the only possibility. When this happens, the only responsible attitude is not to try to explain it away but to allow it to present its own challenge to faith. The experience of our Lord may lead us to believe that honest doubt does not truly lead to despair but only to a deeper faith, but that should be clearly recognized for the act of faith it is. We dare not take it for granted that it will always necessarily be so, with the result that our wrestling with doubt becomes a sham fight. The proper ministry of the man of faith, therefore, to his fellow who seems to be overwhelmed with a 'doubt unto despair' is not to try to act as a Job's comforter but to watch humbly without allowing his own eyes to become heavy.

4. *New Tasks for Christian Thought*

It is of the greatest importance for the Church today that her theologians should accept fully the discipline of doubt as part of their task. They do not need to do this chiefly for apologetic purposes—if they do, their doubt will quickly become dishonest—but in order that they themselves and the Church they serve may find true faith and discover the will of God. We have seen a widespread theological revival in our time, for which we may be grateful. But this revival can become self-defeating unless its limitations are clearly seen. It provides us with no more than the resources with which to set out upon our task in the modern world. It has only gone a little way in the direction of showing us how to fulfil that task, partly because it has even yet not shown itself sufficiently aware of how new and strange the territory is in which we have to move.

Theology, for example, has not yet adequately come to terms with the fact that we live in a physical universe which is immensely larger than previous generations of men could ever have envisaged. The fact itself is familiar enough, but we find it extremely hard to get our imaginations around it. If this planet is one tiny speck in an almost infinite universe, the mystery of human existence is clearly deepened. All previous knowledge of God and of the human situation is far from being necessarily set aside by this knowledge but it obviously has to be looked at in a different perspective. This can hardly be said to have been done. Honest doubt demands that we do so. Otherwise, we may be resisting the call of the Spirit of the living God through fear that expanding knowledge will prove that, after all, he is not the creator of the heavens and the earth.

In the same way, we are being compelled to move into new territory by the great advances made in men's ability to control themselves and each other through the human sciences and those closely related to the human sciences, through psychology, physiology, biology and the rest. We are only at the beginning of these advances and their actual achievements often turn out to be less than the more optimistic claims made for them but, on any showing, they create delicate and difficult problems for the future of mankind, which will require great courage and humility for their solution. So far, theology has not shown as much zeal as it might in meeting this situation.

On a different level, the relation between Christian faith and the other positive religions of mankind appears to invite fresh consideration. Here again it is easy to exaggerate and this large subject, more than most, encourages people to make sweeping and over-confident generalizations. What the precise relations between Christian faith and the other religions should be it may not be given to us to know and only those who have intimate understanding of more than one religion can be expected to have any views which are worth heeding on the matter. But in the light of the greatly enlarged picture of humankind's place in the physical universe and of man's inner life which we now possess, it is hard not to believe that important revision of traditional attitudes, both 'liberal' and 'conservative', about these relations is overdue.

The Church's theologians will not find the courage to venture into the unknown in these realms, and the Church's members will not find the courage to achieve 'holy worldliness', unless they all keep constantly before them the supreme example of Jesus Christ, the Lord of the Church. In his humanity, he, above all men, ventured into the darkness of the unknown in faith. If anyone trusted in the God above God, it was Jesus Christ as he went up to the Cross. From the point of view of historical continuity, the Cross represented the death of God as he had come to be understood in the tradition of Israel. The dead do not praise God, and one who dies outside the city, rejected by the custodians of the Law and in a manner which marks him as a scandalous outlaw, is clearly one who trusts in a God different from the God in whom other men said they believed.[1]

It is true, and it is important to bear this in mind in its proper place, that our Lord saw his vocation in terms of the religious vocation of Israel, which he re-interpreted, and that he could appeal to a more authentic tradition than could his opponents, but that very appeal was itself part of his act of faith. As our Lord went up to the Cross God gave no sign that he was on his side rather than on that of his opponents. Whatever we make of our Lord's enigmatic cry of dereliction, it must mean that God as he had come to be known by Israel was no longer visible, and that any further revelation of him must come from beyond that expression of his nature.

We must see in the light of the Cross that the idea of God which the old Israel had come to hold, which is the idea all religious men who resist the ultimate venture of faith come to hold, went into the shadow of death with Christ, and did not re-emerge. This does not mean that we can learn nothing of God from the Old Testament. The tension between the true God and the images which men make of him is present there also. But it does mean that the God who always speaks from beyond, and who judges all our religious pretensions, and who constantly impels us to scrutinize and revise the ideas we have about him, is the

---

[1] See Bonhoeffer, *Letters and Papers from Prison*, p. 163: 'Our coming of age forces us to a true recognition of our situation vis-à-vis God. God is teaching us that we must live as men who can get along very well without him. The God who is with us is the God who forsakes us (Mark 15.34). The God who makes us live in this world without using him as a working hypothesis is the God before whom we are ever standing. Before God and with him we live without God. God allows himself to be edged out of the world and on to the Cross. God is weak and powerless in the world, and that is exactly the way, the only way, in which he can be with us and help us. Matthew 8.17 makes it crystal-clear that it is not by his omnipotence that Christ helps us, but by his weakness and suffering.'

God who speaks through Christ in the Spirit, and is the God with whom we have now to deal. He allowed Jesus to enter the darkness of the dereliction and to think that he had forsaken him, but in the event he vindicated Jesus' faith. This gives us courage to face whatever doubts and difficulties may confront us without seeking to evade them. He will not ask us to go into any deeper darkness than that into which his own Son went. It is craven lack of trust in him to shrink from our own darkness, however deep it may seem, because we fear that his light will not penetrate it. The God above all our gods has shown in the cross and resurrection of Christ that he exists and that he is more powerful than all those forces in the universe which deny him. He calls us to test the power of those forces to the full that we may prove, and prove anew, that 'He is mighty to the casting down of strongholds and of every high thing exalted against him' (II Cor. 10.4).

IV

The Man of Faith and the Secular Order

1. *The Church and the World*

RELIGION, as man's aspiration after God and as his response to him, thrusts him into a realm beyond the superficial appearance of every day. It makes him aware of the claims of another world than that conditioned by space and time and of other purposes than those which present themselves naturally to him in the midst of his secular occasions. It sets a question mark against all his buying and selling, his marrying and giving in marriage, and asks him, 'What doth it profit a man if he gain the whole world and lose his own soul?'

That this is a proper function of religion our Lord's own teaching and example make clear, but that function is fulfilled only if, as we have seen, religion is constantly transcended in the obedience of faith. Unless this happens, religion achieves its own form of secularization and becomes conformed to this world which passes away. This is the more deadly because religion so readily creates a world of its own, which is neither the real world in which faith lives nor the mixed and confused world of every day. This is what might be called the 'Sunday' world, the world of the Church and its fellowship and of the institutions which express and support these.

The protest on behalf of 'holy worldliness' has arisen because of the weakness and failures of this 'religious' world and the main purpose of the rest of our discussion

will be to try to show how much the Church needs to see
its limitations and organize its life so as to overcome them.
Let it be made quite clear that we are not saying that this
world of religion has no right to exist or that it is necessarily
evil. Just as religion is inescapable, so is its special world.
And in the Christian dispensation, where religion is redeem-
able, there can be a reasonable expectation that, to put it
very mildly, this will be a good rather than a bad world,
one whose life is a genuine testimony to the reality of God,
the Lord of the Church. It is, of course, right and fitting that
believers should approach worship and the community life
of the Church on the Lord's Day in the spirit of Psalm 122
and the hymns of Isaac Watts. To see 'holy worldliness'
simply as a way of depreciating the Church in its consciously
Godward direction is the surest way of ensuring that our
life in the world will have no holiness about it.

Religion in Christ can be good and the world of religion
can be good, but only if religion is fulfilled and that world
is constantly renewed by faith expressing itself in love. This
fulfilment and renewal are impossible unless it is clearly
recognized that the world of religion is part of the life of
men on this earth and can become secularized as readily as
any other world, despite the religious labels affixed to everything within it. It is not a 'sacred' world, operating according to different laws from the so-called 'secular' world outside. It is part of the secular world where it should be possible for the holiness of the people of God to find more
ready and more developed expression than in other places,
but it is not different in kind from other parts of the
secular world. The protagonists of holy worldliness are right
in saying that the process of false secularization has overtaken large parts of the ecclesiastical world of religion in
our own time and that Christian people need radically to
alter their attitudes and procedures in the light of this fact.

It is always difficult to speak precisely of the relation between the Church and the world because the 'world' is used in several different senses in the New Testament. Two different words, *aeon* and *kosmos,* are those most commonly translated the 'world', and they have different shades of meaning. *Aeon* normally refers to 'the world' as this present age, in which life is dominated by 'the rulers of this present age', under whose dominion it is passing away into nothingness, being driven to self-destruction. The Christian claim is that into this *aeon* another order of reality has broken, that of the age to come in which Christ is Lord and the power of the rulers of this present age is broken. Those who live by the laws of this order of reality are able to place upon this present age, as it passes away, the sign of God's kingly rule. They are able to live in the midst of this present world as those who are not of it, and are transformed into the image of the age to come.

The other sense of the word 'world' is, however, the more common. It is that of what we call the material world, especially the earth as the abode of man. This might be described as the characteristic Old Testament sense and it is of the world in this sense that we are most commonly thinking when we speak of the secular order. Even when the word is used in this sense, it is not without an awareness of alienation. This is so acute that the word *kosmos* is used almost in the sense of *aeon* in the Johannine writings. It is clearly important that we should hold these two senses together, because they are so often separated in the minds of many people, with resultant confusion in our understanding of the relation between the Church and the world. The present age in which we are set is evil. The earth as the habitation of man is infected with this evil but it remains God's creation. In overcoming this present age, God releases man for his service as his priest in the creation.

Those who are called out of the world in the sense of existence lying in the hands of evil powers and doomed to self-destruction are able to walk together in church order by the power of Christ through the world in the sense of the creation. Again, church order in this context obviously means something more fundamental than institutional organization. It means the shape which the lives have of those who are overcoming their tendency to slip into the disorder that conformity to this world which passes away brings with it and who are set in the way of being renewed by the power of the world to come, which does not pass away and abides for ever. It cannot be too strongly emphasized, however, that this renewal means the very opposite of being made remote from reality in the present moment. Those who imagine that living by the power of the age to come carries this remoteness with it are not thinking of it in the proper way. They are thinking of the age to come in terms of the Hebrew *Sheol*, where life continues only as a pale, flickering and temporary shadow of what it was on earth. But the life of the age to come is free from the corruption, failure and self-destructiveness which mark life on earth. It is life in which earthly vitality and beauty are purified, glorified and fulfilled, not denied. It is also life centred in God, who loved us when we were dead in trespasses and sins and who identified himself with men in their needy worldliness, as sin was working death in their lives. The Fourth Gospel, which speaks in one breath of the world lying in the power of the evil one, speaks in the next of God so loving the world that he gave his only-begotten Son, that whoever believes in him should not pass away to nothingness but possess God's own enduring life. It stands to reason, therefore, that the fruit of this renewal should be not withdrawal from the world but mastery over it and effective action within it. It is the action of those who, in the midst of trouble, can be of good cheer because Christ has overcome the world. It is also an action of identification on the part of Christ's servants with those who struggle in the world, as Christ identified himself with them, so that, in the midst of their struggles, they can yet experience and enjoy the freedom and spontaneity of the children of God.

It follows from this that when people who bear a Christian name withdraw from what are normally considered to be secular occasions into the circle of religious activities, it is essential that they should know exactly what they are doing. If they imagine that the world, in the pejorative sense, cannot reach them when they are engaged upon these activities—because they are safely established within a religious enclave which can be kept pure and unspotted—they are obviously mistaken. A withdrawal in that spirit is nothing more than a capitulation to the forces of the world in a religious guise. It covertly accepts the fact that the world is too strong to be overcome, in much the same way as theology tries to avoid the challenge of doubt, and hence it is a particularly deadly form of disobedience. It is not an accident that the life of so many of the self-consciously pious enclaves of people who imagine that they have successfully contracted out of most of the evils of ordinary society in this world should be so notably narrow, repressive and stuffy. There are many such societies bearing a Christian name, both Protestant and Catholic, and the fact that the life they produce is so unsatisfactory, not least in the very self-satisfaction it produces among those who live it, is a challenge to Christian understanding and an obstacle to Christian belief which should be recognized and confronted more openly than it often is. The life of these societies is so unsatisfactory because it is frequently a form of worldliness masking itself as unworldliness. It is not for us to say that true holiness is not to be found in their midst, as it is in other societies bearing a Christian name, but these societies do not provide as favourable an environment for its nurture as they imagine because their temptation is to see their obedience to God largely in terms of a limitation of commitment. Their characteristic tendency is to try to restrict the life of the senses as much as possible. When they engage in business activity or politics or even education, they are reluctant to envisage them as spheres where their decisions are affected by their Christian understanding, except in quite secondary ways. While few of them would formally deny that God is to be obeyed along the whole range of life, in practice they assume that he is Lord only over what their conventions have led them to suppose to be the appropriate sphere of religion. They compensate for this limitation by showing great emotional intensity over their religious activities and trying to pay as little attention as possible to what they conceive to be the non-religious aspects of life.

Withdrawal into the sphere of religion from what are commonly called 'secular' occasions is certainly essential, but only as one part of the movement of withdrawal and advance, of gathering and scattering, which produces the characteristic rhythm of the life of those who are in the world and not of it and are moving towards their eternal home. It is typified by the relation between the Lord's Day and the rest of the week in the Christian dispensation. As a fundamental ordinance of God, the Sabbath of the old Israel has been abolished. God has made all meats clean; he has removed the distinction between sacred and secular days. Yet most Christians also believe that God has himself appointed means of grace for his people in Word and sacraments, and they have always been conscious of the need for set seasons in which they assemble and meet together to give thanks and praise, to offer prayer and to build up each other in the faith. In every generation, therefore, they have found it appropriate and convenient to meet on the first day of the week, the day of the Lord's resurrection. But to do this is a human, a secular decision. It is true that it has now the authority of long-established custom behind it and the onus of proving the need to change from it rests upon those who might wish to do so, but as a decision it does not differ in kind from other secular decisions. If the Lord's Day is put on an entirely different plane from the other days of the week, the attention of the Christian community is focused upon the wrong objects and the Lord's Day is turned from a source of blessing into an obstacle to faith in the same way as the Sabbath became in the time of our Lord.

We may cordially agree with Eugen Rosenstock-Huessy[1] that modern men, faced with the strenuous demands of life in the world which they have created for themselves, need even longer and more profound periods of Sabbath repose and refreshment than their predecessors did. Business executives, politicians, professional men and parsons need sabbatical years much more than professors, and need to use them more imaginatively. Yet we must insist that these periods of withdrawal are for the sake of more effective engagement. They do not take men into another world but into a different part of the same world, which has its own temptations as well as its own opportunities. In the same way, the monastic calling may have even more validity today than it has had in earlier times, but only if it is clearly acknowledged that those called to the 'religious' life may lead a more 'regular' but not necessarily a more holy life than those who lead a 'secular' life. Both have different functions within the Body, which supplement each other.

[1] See his prophetic book *The Christian Future*, 1947 (SCM Press), pp. 202-9.

The Church as a visible institution alongside others in the world is essential. It is also sometimes necessary for the Church to express herself in elaborately organized forms. But these can quickly become a conspiracy against God unless the Church recognizes the insidiousness of her temptation to lead her members in a religious retreat from faith. Instead of thinking of itself as primarily an instrument of mission and ministry (in Kraemer's phrase), the Church easily becomes an end in itself. It no longer thinks of its function as subordinate to the divine purpose for mankind and is not prepared to lose its secular identity in service of its neighbour but concentrates on building its own worldly empire, which remains worldly even though it may be adorned with all manner of religious symbols. The most striking proof of the ease with which the Church can succumb to this temptation is provided by the prevalence within its midst of clericalism. Clericalism may be defined as the effort to mark out and establish a world of religion which is to be distinguished from the other areas of life, where decisive power lies in the hands of a self-perpetuating corporation of religious experts.

Clericalism is to be found in varying degrees in all churches, and should be recognized as the characteristically ecclesiastical manifestation of false secularism, of conformity to this world which passes away. Catholicism, especially in its Roman form, provides the most fully articulated example of this, but even churches which try to resist the dangers of creating clerical castes do not escape its influence. The elaborate ecclesiastical apparatus of Protestant churches is designed to serve and sustain the members of the Christian community as they seek to fulfil their mission in service in the daily life of the world, but this apparatus often becomes an end in itself almost as readily as it does in Catholicism. It is one of the ironies of history that churches, which proclaim their belief in the Fall and original sin and insist that the warfare against sin will continue while this earth remains, should frequently be less aware of the corrupting influence of power than states. The dangers of clericalism can be mitigated by devising church constitutions which define and limit the powers of the clergy, but the only real safeguard is that clergy and people should recognize that the scattering of Christ's people in the world is as important as its gathering into church order if it is to fulfil its Christian obedience.

Here indeed is the only way in which the ideas lying behind the phrases 'religionless Christianity' and 'holy worldliness' are ever likely to find any significant expression. A religionless Christianity may strictly be impossible but a church which does not transcend its religion in the venture of faith is the abomination of desolation standing where it ought not, and therefore a sign of the imminence of the End. And that faith always works through love is as true for the institution as for the individual, even though the love may have sometimes to take more complex forms in the case of the institution. It follows from this that true holiness in the world arises only when the members of the Church forget their corporate interest in themselves as participants in an earthly institution as they fulfil their common mission. That mission is fulfilled only in ministry, in identification with the Church's Lord as he identifies himself with men and gives them his redemptive power in their real lives on earth. The action of the Church is sheer unholy worldliness, however much it may be dressed up in religious garb, unless it is covered with the holiness of Christ, and Christ is always found on this earth in the form of a servant. The element of separation which is always bound up with holiness is achieved only as the members of the Church exercise a self-forgetting ministry to their neighbours, as their neighbour's human need is seen in the light of Christ. This is the paradox of holy worldliness in the form of a servant (Phil. 2.7), that separation unto God is achieved only by identification with one's neighbour under God.

2. *Man's Coming of Age*

All this may seem to add up to little more than one of the most familiar truths of Christian experience. Yet the insights of Barth and Bonhoeffer have shown that it possesses implications for understanding the Christian faith and living the Christian life today which are far from being familiar. For the churches, even while they pay eloquent tribute to ideas such as those expressed in the last paragraph, often continue to demonstrate in practice their confusion about what their relation to the world should be. If society outside the Church misunderstands the Church, the Church also misunderstands that society. H. H. Kraemer quotes a saying of the elder Blumhardt, 'Every Christian needs two conversions, first to Christ and then to the world.' Dr H. H. Walz has shown how the evils of clericalism and of what he calls secularism depend upon and nourish one another. The 'autonomy' announced by secularism is the world's misunderstanding of itself. The 'heteronomy', the control from outside which clericalism would like to exercise over all men's lives, is the Church's misunderstanding of the world. In clericalism, the Church usurps the place of the world; in secularism, the world usurps the place of the Church.[1] We may take it that here Dr Walz means by 'the world' the general life of society outside that of the institutional life of the Church.

What happens in this situation is that when particular areas of life which used to be under direct ecclesiastical control become autonomous, it is immediately assumed by

[1] H. H. Walz in *The Ecumenical Review*, April 1958, p. 282.

many churchmen that this represents a victory for faithless secularism. This may be so, however, only on clericalist assumptions. It is true that this autonomy can be achieved in such a way that God's lordship is denied, but the possibility must be reckoned with that it could be achieved in such a way as to express true Christian maturity in freedom. As we shall see, this may prompt a revaluation of much activity in the modern world which is commonly deplored as secularization and indicate a different strategy for churches in relation to other institutions.

The guiding principle for Christians in this realm is that of identification. They will recognize that they are part of the world Christ came to save and that they cannot participate in his saving act unless they do so at those places in the world where they live alongside their fellows, whether their fellows bear a Christian name or not, and where they have to take those decisions which are most significant for their own lives and for the lives of others who depend upon them. This means that, except for that small minority among them who are called to do so for the sake of the whole, they cannot make it the goal of their endeavour as Christians to retreat into the world of specifically religious activities and reduce their contacts with mundane affairs to a minimum. In so far as the minister of the Word and sacraments acts in a representative capacity on behalf of his fellows, he does so in virtue of his sympathetic identification with his fellows in the world as he tries to help them discover God's will, and not of his separation from them as one who leads a special kind of religious life. A measure of separation certainly exists, and it has its own hazards and privileges, but it is not the source of any holiness which the minister may possess. In the same way, the Christian community as a whole is separated from the rest of mankind in virtue of its particular calling and has peculiar perils and opportunities in its internal life which are denied to those who remain outside its fellowship, but its primary task is not to embellish the earthly form of the Church as one institution among others. It is to make manifest the transforming power of Christ in the life of mankind every day, through the institutions of the family, the school, the state, the industrial organization and all the others which make up the fabric of the life of mankind.

It follows from this that Christian action in society must not be thought of as an attempt first to try to discover the will of God through the worship and fellowship of the Church as a distinct institution and then to fulfil that will as best the believer can in the wider life of society, remaining as much as possible under the direction of the church authorities and acting as much as possible in their name. The believer must try to discover the will of God both in the life of the Church and in the various spheres of his secular calling. Christ meets him (in the Spirit) in the Bible, the preaching, the sacraments and the fellowship of the Church, but he also meets him no less in the Spirit at all places where he has to take a decision which significantly determines his own and his neighbour's conduct, whether in work or in the public life or in private personal relationships. Christ in the Spirit does not meet him less readily or fully in these situations than he does in the domestic life of the Church; the difference lies chiefly in the context.

It is true that these different kinds of meeting depend upon each other. Biblical revelation, which is the focus of the attention of the Christian community in church is, together with that community's experience of the ways of God throughout the ages, an indispensable point of reference for the believer in trying to discover God's will in his own situation. As such, it has an essential primacy. But the believer does not need the formal intervention of the Church as an institution before God's will can be disclosed to him. The Spirit of God in Christ is not the possession of the ecclesiastical institution. Since the Ascension, the Spirit is shed abroad among men and it is the task of the ecclesiastical institution not to dispense but to discern and follow its working. When it does this, it becomes a channel of the Spirit's operation and a great help to the believer in discovering the Spirit, but only when it clearly recognizes that the Spirit speaks to men outside its confines. In every situation, the responsibility for discovering and obeying the will of God rests upon the man who has the obligation of decision in that situation and the promise of the Gospel is that he can have the freedom and the power to discern and to obey that will.

It is this conviction of the primacy of God through Christ in the Spirit which lies at the root of the idea expressed in the phrase, 'the relative autonomy of the secular'. The word 'secular' is not, perhaps, the most appropriate in this context because the Church has no monopoly of the 'sacred' and because, as an institution, the Church is as secular as any other, belonging to this present world and subject to the same natural influences which affect all institutions in this world. This is true even though it is also true that the Church is unique among institutions in trying as its primary aim to keep men in communion with and moving toward the world to come. But what the phrase is normally taken to mean is right; that the other institutions, while they are related to and in many ways depend upon the Church, are answerable not to the Church but to the Lord of the Church for the way in which they conduct themselves. For the Church to threaten the secular autonomy (in this sense) of the realms of politics or education or the arts or science or industry is to deny the freedom of the Christian man and to run the risk of rude hands being laid upon the secular autonomy of the Church. People come to resent being dictated to about their affairs by the representatives of an institution who, in their view, do not know how their own institution should function properly. When churchmen quickly assume in this kind of situation that the representatives of other institutions are simply resenting the claims of God upon their lives, it is safe to conclude that those churchmen have succumbed to the temptations of clericalism.

It is true, of course, that this autonomy can easily lead to secularism in the bad sense. What we are concerned to emphasize here is that it is not true that clerical or a more general ecclesiastical control of the other institutions of society provides an effective safeguard against this happening. The only way in which secularism can be avoided in the decisions taken by Christians in the wider life of society is the same as that which enables them to avoid it in the inner life of the Church, by self-transcendence through the commitment of faith. The man in the situation has to accept the fact that the decision is his and that it always confronts him in terms which are never exactly the same as those of previous decisions. The one constant factor is that the God who has revealed himself in Christ requires him to act faithfully even though he has no precedent to guide him and even though there may be few fellow-Christians who can help him. He has the burden of the freedom of the Christian man. The hand of God may not be easily discernible, especially if the realm is one like politics or industry where men have not been accustomed to look for the hand of God or where decisions are extremely complex or highly technical, but this does not remove his obligation to search for it. If he does so with self-criticism, patience and charity, he can be humbly confident that God will bless his efforts and use them in the fulfilment of the divine purpose.

It is, perhaps, in this context that we can best understand Bonhoeffer's idea of the 'coming of age of man in the modern world'. Again, this was an idea he was unable to develop. He obviously referred partly to the significance of the discovery of scientific method and the large measure of control which this gives man over nature, including some aspects of human nature. But he also meant more than this. Modern men have 'come of age' in the sense that they recognize that they are no longer under tutors nor under the control of the rulers of this world but are called to freedom and responsibility. They do not need religion in the limited sense which Bonhoeffer means when he speaks of it, nor are they able to live for long on the basis of dictatorship about how they should behave by institutions for which they hold uncritical reverence. They are compelled now to live with their freedom. They are the heirs of the Messianic kingdom and have been compelled to enter into some of the privileges and responsibilities of their heritage. This has been true ever since the Ascension and Pentecost, but has become much more urgent and obvious since the emergence of the modern world with its combination of intense personal awareness with the enlargement of man's powers. The coming of age of man means that he cannot live any more with the gods. He can only find the fulfilment of his freedom in bond-service of Christ or drive himself to destruction with ever-increasing speed.

3. *The Church's Obligations to Her Members*

We have seen that the primary responsibility for Christian obedience in the world rests with those individuals or groups who are most directly involved in particular situations, and that churches must be careful to respect the relative autonomy of other institutions. But this does not mean that the Church as an institution has no general obligation to her members in the world. On the contrary, she has a very considerable obligation. There are three aspects of it which are not clearly seen by many churches at present.

The *first* is that, in highly developed societies, *the influence of the Church as one secular organization upon other secular organizations should be indirect*. This should be so, not as a simple matter of tactics, but as a matter of principle. In the ordinary way, members of churches should influence the life of other organizations as committed members of those organizations, who claim no privileges for themselves or for their own opinions because they bear a Christian label and who are careful to respect the integrity under God of the organization which they serve. The method of the Communist cell or of the MRA group, that of exploiting the organization for the purposes of its own ideology, should be utterly alien to the Christian in a free society.

Christians should be distinguishable in the general life of society in two ways. The first is by their sense of mission, that is their ability to perform their work in such a way that its relation to God's wider purpose for mankind as defined by Jesus Christ becomes clear and significant. The other is by their ministry, that is by their willing, joyful and self-forgetful service. It is service not primarily of the organized Church or the Christian cause as one particular worldly interest among others, but of their fellow-men through the work itself. The cry 'let the Church be the Church' has, properly, become one of the watchwords of the ecumenical movement; but its corollary is that Christian men should also be eager to enable the university, the school, the government department, the factory and the sports club to fulfil their own function under God. They should not, under the guise of zeal for the Lord's house, greedily try to subsume these functions under that of the Church.

An obvious illustration will make the point clearer. The institutions which bear the closest relation to churches and which are most susceptible of clerical or ecclesiastical control are schools and colleges. A very large number of these, both in America and Europe, grew up as professedly Christian institutions directly under the control of church bodies, generally with clergymen as their headmasters or presidents. In these days many of the most successful of them—in Protestant communities probably the majority—have ceased to be controlled directly by churches and to have clerical heads. This process is often described as secularization and duly deplored as such. It is true that what has happened is often deplorable. The institution may have become hostile to the Christian way of life, may refuse to study Christian theology and may make it difficult for an effective Christian community concerned to obey God through its work to come into being within its walls. But it is wrong to suppose that the reason for this kind of secularization is that the control over the institution's life has passed from church bodies to a new body specially appointed for the purpose. For a school or a college founded by Christian institutions now to become independent and to choose its own officers and decide its own policy may, in itself, be only an indication that it has now achieved its own maturity, that it has 'come of age'.

We do not wish to be misunderstood here. It is good that the initiative in founding educational establishments should come from churches. It is a matter of profound satisfaction that so many should have started in this way and it is a sign of weakness and lack of identification with the needs of society that, in the present period of great educational expansion, churches should not be showing more enterprise in this respect. It is also understandable that, in their early days, schools and colleges should lean heavily on the insti-

tutional strength of churches for their support and upon the
enthusiasm for education of church members for their in-
spiration. But it is no less understandable that, as these
schools and colleges grow in strength and assurance, Christian men within them, no less than other men, should desire
freedom for them to develop according to their own genius.
The principle of true Independency or Congregationalism
in churchmanship has its application to other institutions as
well, as it must if there is any truth at all in what we have
been saying about holy worldliness. Always provided it has
all the equipment necessary for acting responsibly as a
Christian community, each particular church has the freedom and the obligation to take its own decisions *within its
own sphere*. So also has each educational institution. The
parallel is not a complete one, and there are wide varieties
of situation which call for many different approaches, but
the basic principle of the right to independence within its
own proper sphere holds for both. To model schools and
colleges upon the Church and to make similar tests of membership for both, or to assume that schools or colleges can
only be thought of as 'safe' from a Christian point of view
when they are brought as directly as possible under ecclesiastical control, is to reveal misunderstanding both of the
Church and of educational institutions and to create a great
deal of unnecessary tension. Religious observance and fellowship will certainly have their place, and it should normally be a large place, in the life of the school or college.
It should be the duty of churches to see that their members
use their opportunities and fulfil their obligations as crea-
tively as possible in these respects. But religious observance
and fellowship will be misdirected and become an enemy
of faith if those concerned with their organization become
more interested in promoting through them the institutional
prosperity of the churches than in showing a reverent un-

derstanding of the nature of the school or college as an instrument in God's service. They will be the first to insist that the school or college must have as much external freedom to be itself as possible, for without this freedom its members cannot adequately discover the will of God in their life together.

The English public (in American terms : private) schools are far from being models of 'holy worldliness' but their history in the twentieth century provides interesting confirmation of the fact that the weakening of direct clerical control does not necessarily mean a greater degree of conformity to this world which passes away. Clerical influence within them is much less pronounced than it was, and it is now the exception rather than the rule for the headmaster to be a clergyman. Yet most of their critics would agree that they are more congenial institutions from a Christian point of view than they used to be. Lay headmasters, indeed, seem to have developed their own characteristic form of Christian piety. To imagine that the overthrow of clericalism must necessarily mean capitulation to evil secularism is to look for the enemy in the wrong place and sometimes to lament as the Church's defeats what should be celebrated as her victories.

While schools and colleges offer the most obvious illustrations of what we have in mind, the same principle applies with varying degrees of complexity in relation to many other institutions where the Church has the opportunity to exercise great influence and where, through a creative initiative of faith, she has been first in the field to meet an urgent human need. Hospitals and social service organizations are cases in point. The fact that these are not controlled by churches, or that their leaders behave like doctors or social workers rather than clergymen, does not necessarily mean that they are conformed to this world which passes away.

It is a fact of considerable significance that an inappro-
priately close connection with church organizations seems
to act as a blight upon many bodies, particularly business
organizations which have grown up as subsidiaries of church
activities. They are not prepared to take financial risks or
enter into large commitments because this might imperil
their parent bodies, and the temptation to use the moral
prestige of the Church as a substitute for efficiency and enterprise often seems to be irresistible. Most churches recognize, although some may do so very reluctantly, that a theo-
cracy is not necessarily the best form of state, but they are
sometimes slow to see that the reasons for this hold also in
the case of other institutions of society where the prospects
of clerical control are less remote.

The *second* aspect of the Church's obligation to its members in the world is that *the Church itself, in order to make
its own vital and distinctive function clearly defined and to
resist the false secularization which besets it as it does all
other organizations, will be careful to specify its own institutional limits and the terms of membership within it.* A
church which sharply distinguishes membership within it
from membership of other institutions of society is likely to
be more effective than one where that distinction is not
clearly made. This might be paraphrased as saying that a
gathered church is likely to have a more effective influence
on secular society than a territorial one were it not that the
matter is rarely as simple as that. In course of time,
churches which set out as gathered communities often become so assimilated to the general life of society around
them as almost to be indistinguishable from that life. At the
same time, territorial churches can develop such strong un-
official gathered communities within them that they can become an effective leaven. But it needs to be seen that the
idea of a gathered church community is integral to a mature

understanding of the nature of the Church, for it is an attempt to acknowledge the true lordship of Christ, the Crown Rights of the Redeemer, in the Church.

The Church belongs not to men but God, and it is God who calls his children into his communion. It follows from this that the primary gathering agent of the people of God is not the evangelistic zeal of church members nor the cultural coherence of the church institution but the Holy Spirit. It is the task of men to discern whom the Spirit has called and to seek, by every possible means, to unite themselves with them in church order. How to discern the Spirit's calling in such a way as to distinguish it from our own ideas is an important and difficult question with which theology has to deal but which, fortunately, need not concern us now. What does need to be clearly grasped, however, is that the Church has constantly to be called into being, replenished and renewed, and that it does not simply exist as a natural fact, operating through the power of its own institutional vitality in a manner calculable by a shrewd administrator. The frontiers of the Church must always be kept open, so that all whom the Spirit truly calls may be free to enter, with the honest acceptance on the part of the Church's watchmen that the Spirit's ways are not as our ways. Where this is done with faithful attention to the scriptural standards of church membership, the Church is armed with one of its chief safeguards against becoming identified with the other interests of society in the wrong way, which often prevents it from speaking prophetically to men about their national or race or class loyalties.

It is, perhaps, worth saying that the 'gathered' church in this sense is not necessarily synonymous with the 'free' church as contrasted with one which is established by the state. It is not inherently impossible for a church gathered in the sense we have defined to be established in relation to the state, although such a relationship always brings its problems along with its advantages and these should be clearly recognized. Experience in Anglo-Saxon countries has also shown that churches which have no formal relation to the state may achieve such close cultural links with the society in which they are set that they become little more than clubs within that society. The precise character of the relation between church, state and other organs of society may well vary from one situation to another and will probably require frequent adjustment. What is essential is that the principle should be firmly grasped that, as the Church and the other organizations of society grow into their own distinctive kind of maturity, they should, as organizations, become more and not less clearly differentiated from each other.

Thus, in periods of social immaturity, where the structures of a society have not become definitely established or where they are in rapid transition from one style of life to another, a defence can be made for a certain confusion of function between the Church and the other organs of society. In certain kinds of patriarchal society, it will obviously not be easy to distinguish between church and state, any more than it was in ancient Israel. It may well have been right, for example, to baptize a tribe when their chief was baptized. It may well be right today, as some missionaries argue, to take a polygamous family organization into the church rather than to try first to establish a form of monogamy for which the people concerned are not psychologically or economically ready. But where the church and the other institutions of society (of which in this context the state is the most prominent) have 'come of age', it becomes a condition of their most effective ministry to one another that, on the organizational level, they should be clearly differentiated from one another. This is true—indeed, we should claim that it is especially true—even where church members are an active majority element in society or where, as happens in the so-called 'welfare state' societies of the West, the spirit and outlook of the Church have had a considerable influence upon that of the state. Christian men in such a situation will be quick to recognize that a church which confuses its function with that of the state and a state which confuses its function with that of the church become equal enemies of the freedom of the Spirit and the integrity of each institution. They will also recognize that a truly 'free' church, which has full freedom to follow the Spirit with no power of coercion and no privileges which cannot be justified on general social grounds, in a truly 'free' state, which serves the well-being and respects the integrity of all its citizens, represents as near an ideal situation as can be achieved on this earth. This is not 'secularization' but maturity.

This principle has a direct bearing upon the *third* aspect of the Church's relation to its members in the life of the world. *A mature church which is, through all its members and not only through its ministers, at grips with its task in the world will be marked by a certain puritanism about its own institutional activity.* Church activities should be marked by simplicity, economy and concentration. They should be the activities of busy and hungry people, who need sustenance for their spirits urgently, but who also need it to be made available for them readily and quickly, and who have little time for over-elaboration. This is not an argument for making church life superficial, so that people can participate in its activities with little effort. Such activities do not really feed their hunger, and they are also the greatest wasters of time. This is an argument against the fussiness, triviality and pretentiousness of church life, which are the greatest barriers to the effectiveness of churches and

the surest of indications that their members are not in earn-
est about their profession.

What the Church needs from its members today is not so
much more of their time and money for the support of ever-
larger and more numerous organizations, as a different
quality of attention. Ministers can do a very great deal to
evoke this by the quality of their own attention to the affairs
of their churches. If they show a proper sense of priorities in
their use of their own time and energy, the more business-like
and responsible of their fellow-members are likely quickly to
respond. This means that ministers will not, for example, regard it as one of their functions to strive after that kind of pul-
pit eloquence which makes people stop and admire them instead of going out to serve God better in the world. It also
means that they will recognize that the temptation to build
empires through the creation of unnecessarily large staffs
and building programmes must be resisted. Once again,
their task is not to make totalitarian claims for the service
of the sanctuary, but to ensure that the Church maintains
her vital rhythm of gathering and scattering, of withdrawal
and engagement. This, in its turn, does not mean that the
Church's life need lack beauty and dignity and stability, nor
that it need be indifferent to its own secular traditions, but
it does mean that it puts first things first. It will not allow
too many devoted church mice to make their nests in the
house of God, and it will not permit itself to become so
occupied with preserving the relics of the past that it is unable to keep up with its children in the present. God's
people are, fortunately, not required to live on iron rations
all the time but, even in times of great institutional prosperity, they will take care to bring up their children in such
a way that they will know how to do so should the need
arise. The Church is an army on the march and the responsible minister will know that its front-line troops are its

ordinary members engaged with the world and that his chief duty is to help them to be maintained in fitness for battle.

All this may seem to imply that the achievement of so-called 'holy worldliness' in the transcendence of religion by faith working through love demands a Protestant conception of the Church, and also one which is closer to the left than to the right wing of Protestantism itself. There is no disguising the fact that this is the implication of our argument. It needs to be said that the more radical forms of Protestantism, always provided that they have possessed a fully developed Biblical theology and a clear understanding of the place of office in the Church, have often in practice shown a better understanding of the relation of the Church to the world than other churches which have been more eager to proclaim their dignity and their prerogatives. Christian standards of conduct have often pervaded the common life of societies which have had strong left-wing Protestant churches more effectively than they have those societies which have lacked such churches, but where the state has made a much more explicit Christian profession; and that is not simply a fortunate historical accident. This observation is, however, expressed in this vague and generalized way deliberately because, while it has its pertinence when we are confronted by the exclusive claims of some churches, it is singularly unprofitable for anyone to try to make much denominational capital out of a fact of this kind. Protestant churches of all kinds have so frequently failed to grasp their own principles, and to live up to them when they have, and Catholic churches have so frequently shown themselves able to overcome the weakness of their clericalism, that the most useful course to pursue at this stage is to try to learn from the successes and failures of each and to acknowledge how much both have to learn which is quite new.

The truth is that all churches stand so much under the judgment of God in this matter that they have a great deal to learn, not only from each other, but also from the way in which non-ecclesiastical institutions conduct themselves. Ecclesiastical self-centredness has often prevented church- men from recognizing that these have sometimes been more Christian in attitude and procedure than churches themselves, partly because of the quiet influence of Chris- tian people in their service. Ministers can learn much about standards of competence and responsibility from the great professions of the Western world. Churches can learn from states how to handle problems of power honestly and openly. Church meetings in Britain can learn some things about how they should conduct their business in a Christian manner from the House of Commons, particularly in its treatment of individual members overtaken in a fault. Some of the large industrial corporations are discovering methods of flexible self-discipline and of defining responsibility which put church organizations to shame. The people of God need to be gathered together into church order for the proper fulfilment of his will, and he blesses them abundantly when they do so, but he speaks to his children in other places than in church and sometimes more pertinently. The Church will only truly be the Church when it sees the whole of life as the scene of God's action, and when it forgets itself in the venture of faith, overcoming the world in the power of the Christ who is Lord over both the Church and the world.

V

Church and Civilization Today

1. *Religious Revival the Enemy of Faith?*

PIQUANCY is given to the discussion of ideas connected with 'religionless Christianity' in these days by the fact that something like a revival of the Christian religion seems to be taking place. This revival, it is true, is much more marked in some places than in others. It appears to be most vigorous, at least on the institutional level, in the USA. But even in Europe there are many signs of awakening religious interest among people who had previously seemed to be indifferent.

The revival has been greeted by many theologians and other spokesmen of the churches with scepticism. This has been particularly pronounced in the USA, where the revival has often seemed to be more impressive in quantity than in quality and where its popular success has sometimes been in inverse proportion to the amount of prophetic power and 'holy worldliness' which have been displayed. This has made those who might reasonably claim a measure of insight into what true prophecy and 'holy worldliness' are— the theological critics—anxious above all else to demonstrate that they are not taken in by the pretensions of this religious revival. Their criticisms of it have, therefore, generally taken the form of pointing out its limitations rather than of evaluating its significance. This, in its turn, has meant that very little effort has been made to consider carefully what the temptations and the opportunities of this re-

vival are and how best they can be met. If our argument so
far has any validity, it will be clear that nothing is more
urgent than that the churches, and those who flock into
them, should not be encouraged to rest content in their religiousness but should be helped, with humility and sympathy, to move on to the transcendence of their religion in
faith.

No widespread revival of religion can automatically be
taken as a genuine manifestation of faith and that this is
particularly true in this instance is manifest from several
points of view. Several writers, of whom Will Herberg in
Protestant—Catholic—Jew (1957) and Martin E. Marty in
The New Shape of American Religion (1959) have gone into
most detail, have exposed the weaknesses of this revival in
the USA, the former in particular emphasizing the extent
to which it can be explained as a cultural reaction to a social
and religious heritage, which takes very similar forms in
relation to widely different religious traditions and which
does not, in itself, possess a very definite Christian content.
It cannot be denied that the great institutional development
of the churches of all kinds in the USA has taken place with
remarkably little evidence of spiritual tension and strain.
The chief effort involved appears often to have been no
more than that of 'packing them in' with sufficient speed.
This is a far cry from the spirit of revival as expressed by
Martin Luther or John Wesley or Jonathan Edwards. And
it has already been noted that it is not a revival remarkable
for its prophetic power. Those who flock into the churches
are among the most conventionally-minded, and occasion-
ally also the most prejudiced, members of society, and the
fruit of their obedience in life has generally proved to be
more predictable than creative. The revival of religion in
Britain since the second World War has been far less widespread than that in the USA, and consequently it has dis-

played far fewer of the characteristics of a mass movement.
But this provides little cause for self-congratulation on the
part of the British churches, for the unexpectedly conservative and unadventurous character of this revival, in nearly
all denominations, suggests that it has far more affinity with
the American revival than the great differences between
them in institutional expression might suggest.

These facts can easily impel us to the conclusion that the
present revival of religion abundantly proves that religion
can be the greatest enemy of faith and, therefore, provide us
with an excuse for leaving the matter there. But it is precisely at this point that we do well to remember the pro
visional character of that observation. It is undoubtedly
essential to remember that membership of a religious institution, or even an active interest in religious matters, is not
the same as justifying faith. There are many in the membership, and perhaps some in the leadership, of the churches
who do not grasp that simple fact. When they fail to do so,
religion does become the greatest enemy of faith. But this
does not mean that all manifestations of religion which fall
short of the act of faith itself must be written off. Once
again, who is it who takes it upon himself to do the writing
off? As we have seen, faith arises more often than not
through religion, and it cannot be ruled out that, on some
levels at least, this upsurge of religious interest may create
the conditions in which, humanly speaking, faith could be
born more easily than in conditions of previously existing
superficiality or misrepresentation. The religious revival in
the Western lands, and especially in the USA, is often a
healthy reaction against the selfish hedonism and passive
indifference which are the characteristic weaknesses of a
prosperous industrialized society. Even if the only decision
taken by many of those who flock into the churches is
simply one to be in favour of religion as a 'good thing', and

of public acknowledgment of God as an appropriate social activity, that is not always to be despised on every level of experience. It could often be a step in the right direction. Church attendance is, of course, far from being the whole of Christian obedience but it is a form of distrust of the power of the Gospel to take it for granted that when people place themselves within sound of it they must necessarily resist or distrust it. More evidence would be available on this point if the Gospel were more faithfully preached than it often is from the prosperous pulpits of the Western world. Yet in their proper anxiety not to fall victims of spiritual complacency, critically minded theologians almost reach the point of believing that the typical flourishing suburban church is, by definition, a conspiracy against God.

That it can become such a conspiracy is certainly a real possibility. The minister radically betrays the people committed to his charge if he takes fashionable religiousness at its face value and concentrates all his energies only upon stabilizing and developing it upon its own terms. Part of the difficulty which confronts him is that he is constantly under pressure, for reasons which do not owe much to ill-will on anyone's part, to do precisely that. Yet he, of all men, will be aware that, to the extent to which this happens, the present 'revival of religion' will do no more than confirm Oswald Spengler's remarkable prophecy of a generation ago, in the *Decline of the West*, when he spoke of the appearance of 'a second religiousness' which is, according to him, the sign that a culture is drawing to the end of the cycle of its life.[1] The present revival shows enough of the conservatism of outlook, the nostalgia for the past, and the stylization which are characteristic of 'second religiousness' to suggest that the possibility that it will evaporate in this way is a

[1] Eng. trans. (Unwin), vol. ii, pp. 310-15. The German original dates from 1918-22.

real one. It must, therefore, be tirelessly insisted that to see
the Church simply as an institution which covers with divine
authority the existing conventions of Western society—or,
still more, as one which protests against what those conventions have become in the name of an older Western cultural
and religious tradition—is to show a radical misunderstanding of the Church's nature. Any revival of religion at this
stage of the history of the West which does not carry with it
'a conversion to the world' and a recognition of the world's
'coming of age' and of the need to discover a new pattern of
'holy worldliness' is likely to be no more than a cultural
'second religiousness'.

The duties of ministers in this situation are clear. They
must not merely debunk the religious revival but patiently
try to lead people through religion to faith, which produces
not merely more religion but also effective action in the
real world. And they must do this with those who may have
come to church only because it is the thing to do in their
circle or because they want a nice environment for the
children. This means that they must maintain a difficult two-
sided attitude. On the one hand, they must honestly reckon
with the possibility that the churches we know may frequently have to be by-passed, or even to die, to make room
for the renewal of the real Church. On the other, they must
recognize their responsibility to, and their solidarity with,
those who belong to the existing churches. All their talk
about 'identification' is self-dramatization unless they see
that it also implies their identification as ministers with
those whom they serve in the Church. Of no group in the
church is it more true than it is of ministers that they will
not be made perfect, in the sense of finding fulfilment and
maturity, without those whom they have been called to
serve.

The radical attitude to the external form of the Church

presupposed in what has just been said does not imply, as Catholic critics of this position allege, the denial of the reality of the Church in this present world and, lying behind that, the denial also of a real coming of God to man in the incarnation of Jesus Christ. The reverse is the case. This is the only understanding of the Church which does justice to the nature of the Incarnation, just as it is the only under- standing of the Church which does justice to the Ascension and to the nature of the Spirit's guidance. The Incarnation is a real coming of God to man but, because of man's sin, God comes only in the form of a servant, who makes clear his power only from beyond the Cross. The Church which lives in the Spirit of the incarnate Christ must also exist in the form of a servant. She realizes her identity as the Church not simply by being there, as though she did not live in this present world and were unaffected by the chances and changes of this mortal life, but by fulfilling her mission to the world through her ministry of overcoming the world's powers by the greater power of the love of God. It is only as she dis- covers that power in the obedience of faith that she comes alive as the Church. In Dr H. H. Walz's words, the Church must recognize that 'its service to the world will be the more effective, the less it defends its own interests and the more it thinks of human society as a whole, of which it is only a part'.[1]

The fact must be faced that this is easier said than done in a society such as that of the USA, where the Church in its various forms has immense opportunities for institutional development and consolidation. Nor is the situation much easier, although it is certainly different, in Britain, particu- larly where the largest church, the Church of England, is concerned. Here the Church receives every encouragement from its own traditions, its legal position and public ex-

---

[1] *Ecumenical Review*, April 1958, p. 285.

pectation concerning its activities, to think of itself primarily in institutional terms. Churches should see that these difficulties are to be understood as among the many subtle ways in which the fundamental difficulty of the rich man who wishes to enter the kingdom of God confronts them. Churches cannot normally evade the opportunity to take responsible advantage of popular success, nor can they, any more than the old Israel could, simply set aside the privileges they have inherited through the faithful labours of past generations. At the same time, their only hope is that they should see the perils which these carry to their very existence and call upon all the resources of the Spirit to avoid them. It is a sad fact that those churches which are most vocal in asserting the corporate character of the Church as the dwelling-place of 'the whole Christ' and which are most ready to apply the term 'the Body of Christ' without qualification to their own institutional form are also those which are disposed to offer the greatest resistance to the idea that our Lord's words about losing one's life to find it, and about the rich man and the kingdom of God, apply as much to the community of the Church as they do to the individual.

2. *The Leaders Needed in the Churches*

Perhaps the greatest need, on the level of their institutional life, of the churches of the Western world at present is a fresh archetype for the church leader. The leader who is wanted is one who sees his task in terms not of developing and consolidating church institutions in such a way that their permanence in their existing forms is safeguarded, but of trying to meet the needs of an expanding Christian community in such a way that the Church retains its mobility and its prophetic power, and therefore its ability to adapt itself to changes in the future. No one can responsibly deny that those needs have to be met, nor that they are formidable. Churches must, of course, plan new building programmes and increase their incomes and, within carefully defined limits, recruit more professional ministers and other full-time workers. Even more urgently, they have to maintain and expand their foreign missions and service projects, together with the elaborate apparatus these demand for their support. They must also face with courage and enterprise the opportunities presented to them to become the centres of community life for the vast new dormitory and suburban areas into which millions of young families are crowding all over the Western world. This is particularly true of rapidly expanding countries like the USA, Canada and Australia, where literally gigantic efforts will be required to provide basic Christian services to cope with their 'population explosions'.[1] It is impossible for anyone who ignores these considerations to think realistically in terms of church strategy. But they make it more and not less essential that the strategy of churchmen should be developed in the light of the principles we have already enunciated.

This means at least two things of great practical importance. The first is that churches, as they expand, should strive to keep their organization as simple and streamlined as possible and train those who staff it to be open and flexible in outlook. Here churchmen need to bear particularly in mind all that has been said about how a religious profession provides no automatic exemption from temptations common to all men in similar situations. As they adapt themselves to meet the needs of a centralized and highly

---

[1] It is soberly estimated that, with luck, the USA may be able to keep its population down to six hundred millions by the year 2050. (See 'The Future Population "Mix",' by Daniel Seligman and Lawrance A. Mayer, Fortune Magazine, February 1959, p. 228.) At present, church membership tends to increase more rapidly than the population as a whole in the USA.

mobile society, it is inevitable that office-work, and the number of officials working in offices, should increase among the churches, as they do in other organizations. Because of this, many of the criticisms which are directed against this development are irresponsible. Yet churchmen of all men should be vigilant to guard against its dangers. They of all people should strive to keep their institutions free from what Peter Drucker calls 'the pathology of organizations'. They should demonstrate that they are not conformed to this world which passeth away by the ease and confidence with which they are able to break Parkinson's various laws, constantly producing leaders who are able to take risks and break precedents, who are not the slaves of fixed rules and stereotyped procedures, who are unconcerned with personal prestige and empire-building and who are more interested in seeing that the job is done than in safeguarding their own careers.

Perhaps it needs to be added that this must not be taken as an argument in favour of that meanness of spirit shown by some church organizations to their servants, where they exploit the loyalty of those who are employed full-time in their service in a manner which the average business corporation would consider reprehensible. Yet it is often the organizations who are worst in this respect who are also the least efficient in more fundamental ways. It is true even on the level of church organizations that those who are prepared to lose their life are those who most frequently find it.

The other thing which the Church must never forget in a period of adaptation and expansion is the danger she incurs if she becomes greedy for secular power. Secular power for the Church nearly always means clerical power. The excessive use of clerical power is likely to stunt and inhibit the proper growth both of the Church and of the other institu-

tions of society which should be in a relationship of creative
inter-action with the growing Church. These are days when,
in many situations, members of churches and, in some situations, church organizations, should be taking the initiative
in founding schools, colleges, voluntary service organizations, political parties, scientific research organizations and
industrial concerns. It is very doubtful whether, for all our
'religious revival', the Christian community is showing as
much vitality as it might in these matters, especially as far
as the so-called under-developed areas of the world are concerned. But these are also days when it is more important
than ever, for their own sakes and for the sake of the
churches, that these institutions should be helped to achieve
their own maturity as quickly as possible, so that they are
able to stand on their own feet and go their own way with
the minimum of dependence on the clergy and upon church
organizations.

The experience over the last hundred years of the
churches in Britain, and in some of the older parts of the
USA, demonstrates vividly the consequences which can
follow when these two principles are not clearly grasped.
In the latter half of the nineteenth century, churches found
themselves in a situation where the tide was with them.
They embarked upon a policy of institutional expansion
with the utmost zest. They created new centres in every new
neighbourhood as it opened up. In an era of acute denominational self-consciousness, they cheerfully duplicated and
triplicated facilities, sometimes doing their best deliberately
to outbuild one another. In some places, such as New York
and Liverpool, they embarked upon grandiose cathedral
building projects in emulation of the Middle Ages and with
magnificent disregard for the practical needs of modern
church life. Churches were then, even more than now, convenient centres for local social activity, and they gathered

around themselves a large network of subsidiary organizations. Much of this activity was necessary, as is the great programme of church building which is demanded in the USA today. Not a little of it was a genuinely creative response to the challenge of what was then a new situation. But it can now be seen that this expansion was not always undertaken in a sufficiently careful and self-critical spirit and that the churches also sometimes acted from a desire for institutional self-aggrandisement in which not all the glory was given to God.

The result of this is familiar. The successors of those who enjoyed Victorian prosperity find themselves with burdens grievous to be borne. This is, in some instances, a matter of diminishing numbers of the faithful having to struggle to maintain pretentiously large buildings in neighbourhoods which have changed, although vigorous leadership can do much to deal with this in a time of rising property values. It is much more one of dealing with the problems created by the continuing existence of large numbers of organizations and activities created under an ecclesiastical umbrella to meet ephemeral demands. These, which were often at best no more than semi-relevant to the Church's real concerns and in which many older people now have a strong vested interest, absorb so much of the time and energy of ministers and members of the churches that they have little left for dealing with their real task in the world of today. It is for this reason as much as for any other that the well-settled Protestant church in an older neighbourhood in Britain or America frequently becomes a distraction rather than a source of help to Christian men concerned to 'overcome the world'. It is not merely that such a church has become an ecclesiastical buffer-state between the Kingdom and the world; even as that it is out of date. It is true that, as sensible church leadership will recognize, there is always a problem of altering old-established organizations to meet changing circumstances. The point is that the lack of a clear understanding in the past of the relation of the Church as an institution to her most important task has made this problem quite disproportionately difficult in the present. It is essential that in the current period of expansion the churches should not make the same mistakes.

This can only be avoided if the Church—and here, in most churches, the responsibility of those in the ministry is peculiarly heavy—resolutely pursues two lines of action which may superficially appear to contradict one another but which are, in fact, essential to each other if the Church is to survive.

First, *it must insist on the primacy and indispensability of the characteristic church actions*, through which the Church maintains decisive contact with the sources of its own distinctive life. Nothing must be allowed to detract from the centrality in the Church's life of faithful preaching, the celebration of the sacraments, the public reading of the Scriptures and the prayers, and from the closely-knit community life in church order which maintains and is sustained by these. A great deal of popular Protestantism in the last few generations has allowed other interests to detract from this centrality, and this has been a major source of weakness to its churches. Much of the strength and attractiveness of Catholicism in the modern world has been derived from the fact that, despite all the handicaps which it imposes upon itself, it has placed the means of grace as it understands them so firmly at the heart of the Church's life.

Protestants will disagree with Catholics about the relation of the various means of grace to one another and about the function of the ministry in connection with them, but many Protestants need to acknowledge that they can learn from Catholics on this point of the primacy given to the means of grace. One of the things they do well to note is that the 'given' quality of the Catholic liturgy, and even, paradoxically, its very archaic quality, may have something to teach them. The same is true, in a less pronounced manner, of the Book of Common Prayer of the Church of England. These liturgies succeed in giving the impression that the worship and message and ministry of the Church are primarily concerned, not with the ephemeral needs of the passing generations, but with the permanent human situation. This has to be qualified by the observation that this impression is greatly strengthened in situations where the Church bears very little relation to a folk culture. In such situations, as in central London or the southern English countryside, people are able to receive the ministrations of the Church in almost anonymous fashion and then to move out strengthened by them into the wider life of the world, without becoming dominated by the 'religious' world of the clergy in any restrictive sense. In places like Ireland, where the Church is deeply involved with a folk culture and has to come to terms with all the manifestations of popular religion, Catholicism finds it at least as hard as does Protestantism to put first things first. But most Protestant churches, and especially those which properly emphasize the importance both of spontaneity in worship and of congregational fellowship, need to re-assert the primacy of the means of grace in the Church's life and to devise ways in which, in a mobile and constantly changing society, they can be prevented from being too much at the mercy of temporary fashions or the idiosyncrasies of particular individuals and groups. The up-to-date expression of today very easily becomes the out-of-date expression of tomorrow, and conservative sentiment gathers around the successfully up-to-date form of worship as quickly as it does around anything else in the religious world. The centrality of the Bible, and emphasis on the importance of having an educated ministry to interpret it, have always been the chief safeguards devised by Protestant churches against this happening, and the importance of these must be re-affirmed, but they need to be reinforced by a clearer understanding throughout the community of the Church of the meaning and function of the sacraments, of what is and is not to be expected from preaching, and what the respective responsibilities of minister and people are in public prayers and in the ordering of the internal life of the Church.

Secondly, however, *the Church and its faithful ministers, having done their best to ensure that the means of grace are available as readily as possible, will strive to keep the Church free from any encumbrances which might prevent it from coming to grips with the world about it*. They will always be cutting away dead wood, always encouraging the Church's members to give priority to service of Christ in the world rather than to the world of religion in which the internal life of the Church moves, even at the expense of the legitimate vitality of that internal life. The minister will have to accept a rôle which is poles apart from that of the successful institutional promoter which is often regarded as normative by many of the flourishing churches of the West today. He may even have to incur the odium of some fellow-members of the Church in doing so. And he will spend a great deal of time and energy in helping his fellow-members see that it is as they approach their task in the world with humility, competence and perseverance that they best serve the Church. It is not easy for the chief executive officer of an institution to have the responsibility of constantly reminding its members that they are called to serve other things which are more important than the secular well-being of that institution, but the minister can approach this task with confidence because he cannot really proclaim the faith which he professes without understanding why this must be so and without seeing ways in which it can be so.

There is no place where religion becomes the enemy of faith more obviously than where the Church becomes pre-occupied with her own institutional stability and with defin-ing her precise position as a centre of power over against the rest of society. History abundantly proves that this temp-tation cannot be avoided simply by staging an anti-institu-tional rebellion. Like political revolutions, such rebellions quickly fall into the same traps as those from which they set out to escape, unless they themselves very clearly recognize that their main problem consists in trying to maintain the life of the Spirit in a situation where a measure of institu-tional life is not only unavoidable but also proper and desir-able. Simply to sweep aside a corrupt institution, although this may sometimes be necessary, is quite insufficient. It is their recognition of this which marks off the achievement of John Owen and many of his fellow-Independents of the seventeenth century from the spiritualizing sects which sur-rounded them and which, for a brief season, must have appeared to possess more vitality. Owen and his colleagues saw the need so to define church order as to make it the instrument of the Spirit, and not merely its regrettable ad-junct or a device for claiming the authority of the Spirit for the authority of men over their fellows. The whole art of churchmanship, and it is appropriate that that word should be thought of as possessing some of the same highly am-biguous and self-conscious connotation that a word like 'lifemanship' does, consists in preventing the Church from becoming an end in itself and in preserving its instrumental character. The institutional form of the Church's life is a necessary expression of that life but it should exist as being 'in but not of' the institutional world, always breaking through the laws which govern that world at the command and in the power of the Lord the Spirit.

3. *The Need for Research and Experiment*

What does this mean in specific terms for the churches of the Western world today, and in particular for those of Britain and North America? It means one thing which is simple, practical and obvious; that these churches should devote far more of their time, money and energy than they are devoting at present to the equivalent in the religious world of research and experiment in the world of technology. To put the matter in more religious language, the Church cannot live as the Church unless she is sending spies out into the unknown territory ahead of her, to view the Promised Land from afar off and to help her so to direct her steps that she might reach it the more quickly. We have emphasized that it must always be one of the chief functions of the ministry in the Church not to be simply the administrators of the Church's temporary camps but to insist that the people of God should keep moving towards their goal. Their expertise should develop more in the direction of being able to strike camp quickly and find their way through unknown country rather than in that of making the camps comfortable and defining their bounds. In a time like the present, where the need to pass through new territory is so great and the landmarks to guide the Church through it are so few, the necessity for the ministry to redefine its function in these terms is particularly urgent.

A great deal of the confusion, frustration and ineffectiveness shown by churches today is due to their relative failure to do this, and if anything is certain, it is that, unless they bestir themselves, they are laying up even more trouble for themselves in the future. This failure is manifest in the theological realm itself where, as we have seen, Christian teaching needs far more re-definition than it has so far received in the setting of the realization that the universe is vastly larger than our forefathers knew and of our greatly increased knowledge of other civilizations and religions, which makes us more acutely aware of the relativity of all foundations of religious experience, including Christian dogmatic ones. The revival of Biblical study and of the study of some limited aspects of church history and the history of Christian doctrine which has taken place in our time should greatly assist the Church in this work of re-definition. It is, however, an example of the religious retreat from faith that, in modern England especially, concentration upon these is being used increasingly as a justification for avoiding the difficulties of the work of systematic theology through which alone that re-definition can be attempted.

The need is no less urgent in relation to discovering a fresh style of life for the Church as a community in our own time. There are many thoughtful Protestants who are acutely dissatisfied with the forms of worship and with the patterns of community life of the churches of which they are members. It is often a mark of the Protestant who has seen some of the meaning of 'religionless Christianity' that he has constantly to make up his mind on Sunday morning whether the irritation which he will experience if he goes to church is less intolerable than the sense of frustration and guilt he will have if he stays at home. This may well be largely due to his own weakness and pride and his inability to make allowances for the circumstances of his neighbours, but it would be a self-confident churchman indeed who would claim that these alone accounted sufficiently for his attitude. The situation does not appear to be as critical in this respect in Catholicism, partly because of the great emphasis laid upon the objectivity of the means of grace and partly because of the psychological effect of the swift re-

bukes bestowed upon all complaints against established
practice by the self-confident clerics with which Catholicism
is plentifully supplied. But a book like François Mauriac's
The Stumbling Block[1] is a revealing sign that differences
between churches in these respects are not more than superficial. All Christians need to make fresh efforts to discover
more satisfactory and easily maintained modes of public
and private worship, of religious education, and of corporate life in the midst of the restlessness and superficiality
which are characteristic of the twentieth century in the West.

There are other places where the need for research and
experiment has long been obvious. We still need to give far
more attention than most of us have been disposed to give
to trying to discover God's will in relation to our immense
technological inventiveness and to the society which technology dominates. Otherwise, few things are more certain than that these gifts will work to our destruction and
not to our advantage. The churches need also to make many
more efforts to reach the industrialized masses of people in
large cities, who are peculiarly resistant to the appeal of
Christian institutions. It is no less important, although fortunately it is also a little easier, to make new efforts to reach
those who lead the characteristic life of metropolitan
centres, including those who, through the control of the
large-scale modern media of communication, do a great deal
to shape the lives and determine the attitudes of most people
in the whole community.[2] Research and experiment along
new lines are also needed in the extremely complex and
delicate task of making contact with, and reaching understanding of, people of other religions and cultures than those
of the Christianized West.

---

[1] Eng. trans., 1947 (Harvill Press).
[2] See Gibson Winter, *The Suburban Captivity of the Churches*,
1961 (SCM Press and Doubleday).

The churches of the Old World need research and experiment if they are to discover how to be born again when they are old. The churches of many parts of the New World need them no less if their rapidly expanding communities are to grow in the right direction. The churches of the USA in particular are shooting up so rapidly that the temptation becomes very strong to allow the process of growth to absorb all their energies and to judge all activities by the extent to which they serve that process. It is vital that this temptation be resisted. To sacrifice long-term needs to the practical necessities of the moment, however urgent they may be, is dangerous to an institution. It is disastrous to churches, and especially to the churches of the USA at this particular stage in their history. What will happen if this sacrifice is made is that, when the present wave of expansion spends itself, people will begin to wonder what happens next, and everyone will have been so busy helping the expansion on its way that no one will be in a position to say. People will then be tempted, with the characteristic conservatism of religious institutions on the defensive, to fall back upon pretending that they are still in a situation of expansion and will carry on in a frenzied manner with activities and procedures which are increasingly irrelevant, while the real movements of the Spirit in their own time pass them by. It is a law of the continuing life of churches that they must deepen as they expand. Otherwise, they evaporate in clouds or petrify into monuments in the next generation.

It is not, of course, suggested that churches are unaware of the need for research and experiment along the lines which have been mentioned. A fair amount is being done in these fields in many places, but it is nothing like enough. Where it exists also, it is often regarded as being marginal to what is still thought of as the 'real' life of the churches.

To put things on a very humdrum level, should churches spend less in proportion to their income on research and experiment than do enlightened industrial firms with a faith in their own future? Peter Drucker has pointed out that industrial research—independently of military research—took 0·1 per cent. of national income in the USA thirty years ago and that, in these days, it takes about 2 per cent. of an income four times as large. He also points out that what he calls 'the research explosion' is still going on.[1] Is the effort made by churches to discover how they can adjust and develop their work in this age of innovation even remotely commensurable with this? New experiments are still frequently looked at askance by 'practical' churchmen and if they show no prospect of producing impressive statistical returns in accordance with existing patterns, the demand that support should be withdrawn from them is quickly heard. Such an attitude is often short-sighted even from the point of view of institutional prosperity; it is certainly the reflection of a radical misunderstanding of the nature of the Church. The ecumenical movement has given a genuinely prophetic lead to the churches in our own time and has called them forward along paths which are clearly enough defined, even though it may require great faith and perseverance to keep to them. To follow these paths, and not to concentrate on denominational consolidation on sites marked out in previous centuries, should be seen as the way for the Church into the future.

Nothing is more necessary for the continuance of churches in obedience to God their Lord than that they should move beyond their existing forms and procedures into the venture of faith. Those who strive to make that venture should, however, always remember that, in making it,

[1] *Landmarks of Tomorrow*, 1959 (Heinemann and Harper), pp. 19-20.

they also are not exempt from the dangers of turning their own relatively enlightened religion into the enemy of faith. The Church may indeed spend too much of her time today in making 'insiders' comfortable but the way to protest against this is not by dramatizing oneself as a more Christian 'outsider'. The true follower of Jesus Christ is neither an 'insider' nor an 'outsider' but one who humbly serves his Lord as he suffers outside the camp, bearing the reproach of all who are within. The churches as they are must be transcended, but they can only be transcended by those who are identified with them. And the way of that transcendence is always the way of charity, both to those who are within and to those who are without. This is the first and the last of the matter. Religionless Christianity or mature faith has been reached only when it has found fulfilment in love.

FROM BONHOEFFER'S LETTERS
(*See note on page 9*)

May 5th 1944

I EXPECT you remember Bultmann's paper on the de-mythologizing of the New Testament? My view of it today would be not that he went too far, as most people seem to think, but that he did not go far enough. It is not only the mythological conceptions, such as the miracles, the ascension and the like (which are not in principle separable from the conceptions of God, faith and so on) that are problematic, but the 'religious' conceptions themselves. You cannot, as Bultmann imagines, separate God and miracles, but you do have to be able to interpret and proclaim *both* of them in a 'non-religious' sense. Bultmann's approach is really at bottom the liberal one (*i.e.* abridging the Gospel), whereas I seek to think theologically.

What do I mean by 'interpret in a religious sense'? In my view, that means to speak on the one hand metaphysically, and on the other individualistically. Neither of these is relevant to the Bible message or to the man of today. Is it not true to say that individualistic concern for personal salvation has almost completely left us all? Are we not really under the impression that there are more important things than bothering about such a matter? (Perhaps not more important than the matter itself, but more than bothering about it.) I know it sounds pretty monstrous to say that. But is it not, at bottom, even Biblical? Is there any concern in the Old Testament about saving one's soul at all? Is not righteousness and the kingdom of God on earth the focus of everything, and is not Romans 3.14 ff., too, the culmination of the view that in God alone is righteousness, and not in an individualistic doctrine of salvation? It is not with the next world that we are concerned, but with this world as created and preserved and set subject to laws and atoned for and made new. What is above the world is, in the Gospel, intended to exist *for* this world—I mean that not in the anthropocentric sense of liberal, pietistic, ethical theology, but in the Bible sense of the creation and of the incarnation, crucifixion, and resurrection of Jesus Christ.

Barth was the first theologian to begin the criticism of religion—and that remains his really great merit—but he set in its place the positivist doctrine of revelation which says in effect, 'Take it or leave it': Virgin Birth, Trinity or anything else, everything which is an equally significant and necessary part of the whole, which latter has to be swallowed as a whole or not at all. That is not in accordance with the Bible. There are degrees of perception and degrees of significance, *i.e.* a secret discipline must be re-established whereby the *mysteries* of the Christian faith are preserved from profanation. The positivist doctrine of revelation makes it too easy for itself, setting up, as in the ultimate analysis it does, a law of faith, and mutilating what is, by the incarnation of Christ, a gift for us. The place of religion is taken by the Church—that is, in itself, as the Bible teaches it should be—but the world is made to depend upon itself and left to its own devices, and that is all wrong.

June 6th 1944

The world which has attained to a realization of itself and of the laws which govern its existence is so sure of itself that

we become frightened. False starts and failures do not make
the world deviate from the path and development it is following; they are accepted with fortitude and detachment as
part of the bargain, and even an event like the present war is
no exception.

Christian apologetic has taken the most varying forms of
opposition to this self-assurance. Efforts are made to prove
to a world thus come of age that it cannot live without the
tutelage of 'God'. Even though there has been surrender on
all secular problems, there still remain the so-called ultimate
questions—death, guilt—on which only 'God' can furnish
an answer, and which are the reason why God and the
Church and the pastor are needed. Thus we live, to some
extent, by these ultimate questions of humanity. But what if
one day they no longer exist as such, if they too can be
answered without 'God'?

We have of course the secularized off-shoots of Christian
theology, the existentialist philosophers and the psycho-
therapists, who demonstrate to secure, contented, happy
mankind that it is really unhappy and desperate, and merely
unwilling to realize that it is in severe straits it knows
nothing at all about, from which only they can rescue it.
Wherever there is health, strength, security, simplicity, they
spy luscious fruit to gnaw at or to lay their pernicious eggs
in. They make it their object first of all to drive men to
inward despair, and then it is all theirs. That is secularized
methodism. And whom does it touch? A small number of
intellectuals, of degenerates, of people who regard themselves as the most important thing in the world and hence
like occupying themselves with themselves. The ordinary
man who spends his everyday life at work, and with his
family, and of course with all kinds of hobbies and other
interests too, is not affected. He has neither time nor inclina-
tion for thinking about his intellectual despair and regarding

his modest share of happiness as a trial, a trouble or a disaster.

The attack by Christian apologetic upon the adulthood of the world I consider to be in the first place pointless, in the second ignoble, and in the third un-Christian. Pointless, because it looks to me like an attempt to put a grown-up man back into adolescence, *i.e.* to make him dependent on things on which he is not in fact dependent any more, thrusting him back into the midst of problems which are in fact not problems for him any more. Ignoble, because this amounts to an effort to exploit the weakness of man for purposes alien to him and not freely subscribed to by him. Un-Christian, because for Christ himself is being substituted one particular stage in the religiousness of man, *i.e.* a human law. Of this more later.

July 21st 1944

During the last year or so I have come to appreciate the 'worldliness' of Christianity as never before. The Christian is not a *homo religiosus*, but a man, pure and simple, just as Jesus was man, compared with John the Baptist anyhow. I don't mean the shallow this-worldliness of the enlightened, of the busy, the comfortable or the lascivious. It's something much more profound than that, something in which the knowledge of death and resurrection is ever present. I believe Luther lived a this-worldly life in this sense. I remember talking to a young French pastor at A. thirteen years ago. We were discussing what our real purpose was in life. He said he would like to become a saint. I think it is quite likely he did become one. At the time I was very much impressed, though I disagreed with him, and said I should prefer to have faith, or words to that effect. For a long time I did not realize how far we were apart. I thought I could acquire faith by trying to live a holy life, or something like it.

Later I discovered and am still discovering up to this very moment that it is only by living completely in this world that one learns to believe. One must abandon every attempt to make something of oneself, whether it be a saint, a converted sinner, a churchman (the priestly type, so-called!) a righteous man or an unrighteous one, a sick man or a healthy one. This is what I mean by worldliness—taking life in one's stride, with all its duties and problems, its successes and failures, its experiences and helplessness. It is in such a life that we throw ourselves utterly in the arms of God and participate in his sufferings in the world and watch with Christ in Gethsemane. That is faith, that is *metanoia*, and that is what makes a man and a Christian (cf. Jer. 45). How can success make us arrogant or failure lead us astray, when we participate in the sufferings of God by living in this world?

KIERKEGAARD ON FAITH

From *Fear and Trembling*, translated by Robert Payne
(p. 48), by permission of the publishers, Oxford University
Press and Princeton University Press. See p. 19 above.

LET me say frankly that I have never, in the course of my
experience, seen a reliable example of the knight of faith,
but I do not for a moment deny that every other man may
be such a knight. Meanwhile I have spent years searching
for him in vain. Men are accustomed to travelling the
world, looking for rivers and mountains, new stars, birds
of gay-coloured plumage, monstrous fishes, ridiculous
races of men; they abandon themselves to an animal
stupor and gaze open-mouthed at life, believing that they
have seen something. None of these things interest me at
all. But if I knew where there lived a single knight of the
faith, I would make a pilgrimage on foot to greet him;
for this is the miracle which occupies my thoughts exclu-
sively. Not for a moment would I let him out of my sight;
I would watch how he performed each movement and consider myself made for life; I would divide my time between watching him and practising the movements he
made, and thus spend all my time in admiring him. As I
have said, I have never discovered a knight of the faith,
but I can easily imagine one. Here he is. I make his acquaintance, I am introduced to him. And the moment I
lay eyes on him, I push him away and leap back suddenly,
clap my hands together and say half aloud: 'Good God!
Is this really he? Why, he looks like an Inspector of
Taxes!' But it is really he. I draw closer to him, I watch
every movement he makes to see whether he shows any
sign of the least telegraphic communication with the infinite, a glance, a look, a gesture, an air of melancholy, a
smile to betray the contrast of infinity and the finite. But
no! I examine him from head to foot, hoping to discover
a chink through which the infinite can peer through. But
no! He is completely solid. How does he walk? Firmly.
He belongs wholly to the finite; and there is no townsman

dressed in his Sunday best, who spends his Sunday after-
noon in Frederiksberg, who treads the earth more firmly
than he; he belongs altogether to the earth, no bourgeois
more so. In him you will find no trace of that exquisite
exclusiveness which distinguishes the knight of the infinite. He takes pleasure in all things, takes part in everything, and everything he does, he does with the perseverance of earthly men whose souls hang fast to what they
are doing. He does his job thoroughly. At first glance you
would think he was a clerk who had lost his soul to
double-entry book-keeping, so punctilious he is. On Sun-
days he takes a holiday. He goes to church. No heavenly
glance, no sign of incommensurability betrays him; and
without knowing him it would be impossible to distinguish
him from the rest of the congregation, for his healthy bel-
lowing of the psalms proves only that he has got a sound
pair of lungs. During the afternoons he walks out to the
woods. His heart rejoices over everything he sees, the
crowds, the new omnibuses, the Sound. If you met him on
the Strandvej, you would think he was a shopkeeper having a good time, his delight being of that kind: for he is
not a poet and I have tried in vain to detect in him any
sign of poetic incommensurability. When he comes home
in the evening, he walks as sturdily as a postman. On his
way he thinks about the special hot dish which his wife
has been preparing for him, a grilled lamb's head gar-
nished with herbs perhaps. If he meets someone similarly
disposed, he is quite capable of walking as far as Østerport
if only he can discuss the dish, and he will discuss it with
a passion which would give credit to a *maître d'hôtel*. As
it happens, he has not fourpence to spare: but he still believes that his wife has a hot meal waiting for him. If she
has, it will be an enviable sight for distinguished people
and an inspiring one for common folk to see him eat; for
his appetite is stronger than Esau's. If his wife has not prepared it he remains—oddly enough—unmoved. On his
way he comes to a building site and meets another man.
They begin talking, and before you can say jack-knife he
has erected a new building, himself disposing of all that is
necessary. The stranger will leave him, thinking he has met
a capitalist, while the knight will be marvelling at the
thought that if it really came to the point, nothing would
be easier. He leans out of the window and looks across
the square in which he lives. He is interested in everything
he sees, even if it is only a rat creeping into a gutterhole

or children playing; he regards life as peacefully as a girl of sixteen. Yet he is not a genius, and I have tried in vain to detect in him the incommensurability of genius. In the evening he smokes his pipe, and to see him you would swear that he was the butcher from over the way, vegetating in the evening twilight. He is as free from cares as any ne'er-do-well, but every moment of his life he purchases his leisure at the highest price; for he makes not the least movement except by virtue of the absurd. And yet— and yet I could become furious at the thought of it, if only out of envy—this man is making and has made at every moment the movement of infinity! In infinite resignation he drains the dark waters of melancholy to the last drop; he knows the blessedness of infinity; he has known the pain of forsaking everything in the world that was most dear to him; and yet the taste of the finite is as pleasing to him as if he had never known anything higher, for he remains in the finite without betraying any sign of his uneasy and tortured training, and yet rejoices in it with so much assurance that for him there appears to be nothing more certain. Yet the whole earthly shape which he assumes is something newly created by virtue of the absurd. In his infinite resignation he gave up everything and then regained everything by virtue of the absurd. He is always making the movement of infinity, but he makes the movement with so much precision and assurance that he possesses himself of the finite without anyone, even for a moment, suspecting anything else. The most difficult feat which a dancer can attempt is said to be to leap and take up a definite attitude, so that at no particular moment does he appear to be trying to take up this position, but assumes the attitude as he leaps. Perhaps there are no dancers who can perform this feat—but the knight performs it. Most men's lives are lost among the joys and sorrows of the world; they 'sit out' and take no part in the dance. The knights of infinite resignation are dancers and have elevation. They make the upward movement and fall down again; and this pastime has much to commend itself, is not unpleasing to the eye. But every time they fall down, they cannot immediately take up their positions, they falter for a moment and their faltering shows that they are strangers in the world. This is more or less apparent according to the degree of their art, but even the most masterly of them cannot conceal his faltering. It is not necessary to watch them in the air, one need only watch them at the moment when they touch and have touched the earth—then you will recognize them. To be able to fall in such a way as to appear at once standing and walking, to be able to transform the leap into life into a normal gait, to be able to express perfectly the sublime in terms of the pedestrian—only the knight can do this—and this is the single miracle.

INDEX